James Bond on Location

Volume 1: London

J. P. Sperati

All correspondence for
**James Bond on Location
Volume 1: London**
should be addressed to:

Irregular Special Press
Endeavour House
170 Woodland Road
Sawston
Cambridge
CB22 3DX

❋❋❋❋❋ O ❋❋❋❋❋

Copyright © 2013 Baker Street Studios Limited
All rights reserved
Typesetting is in Times New Roman font

ISBN: 1-901091-56-2 (10 digit)
ISBN: 978-1-901091-56-4 (13 digit)

> Deluxe full colour edition also available
> ISBN: 1-901091-55-4 (10 digit)
> ISBN: 978-1-901091-55-7 (13 digit)

Proof reading & editing: Roger Johnson
Back cover: The SIS Building at Vauxhall Cross

❋❋❋❋❋ O ❋❋❋❋❋

All rights reserved. No part of this publication may be reproduced, stored in a retrieval system, or transmitted, in any form or by any means, electronic, mechanical, photocopying, recording or otherwise, without the prior permission of the Irregular Special Press.

❋❋❋❋❋ O ❋❋❋❋❋

This publication is not part of the official James Bond series. It has not been endorsed or authorised by EON, Danjaq, LLC, United Artists Corporation, Columbia Pictures Industries, Sony or MGM. It does not claim or imply any rights to the Ian Fleming characters or creations and is a historical review of those locations already in the public domain used in filming the James Bond series. Film titles, character names and other information that might be copyright protected are used for reference only.

❋❋❋❋❋ O ❋❋❋❋❋

Every effort has been made to ensure accuracy, but the publishers do not hold themselves responsible for any consequences that may arise from errors or omissions. Whilst the contents are believed to be correct at the time of going to press, changes may have occurred since that time or will occur during the currency of this publication.

For James,
James A. E. R.

For James.

CONTENTS

Introduction 7
James Bond in London 13
    Borough of Barnet 13
    Brent Cross – Brent Cross Shopping Centre 13

    Borough of Camden 17
    King's Cross – St. Pancras Station 17

    Royal Borough of Greenwich 21
    Greenwich – Old Royal Naval College 21
    North Greenwich – The O2 24

    Borough of Hackney 26
    Stoke Newington – Kingsland House 26

    Borough of Hillingdon 28
    Harefield – Summerhouse Lane 28
    Ruislip Gardens – R.A.F. Northolt 29

    Borough of Hounslow 34
    Feltham – Bedfont Lakes Office Park 34

    Royal Borough of Kensington & Chelsea 36
    Fulham Broadway – Brompton Cemetery Chapel 36
    Imperial Wharf – Snake Ranch Studios 38
    Sloane Square – Cadogan Square 40
        Miscellaneous Locations 42
        Sloane Square – Wellington Square, Henniker Mews 42

    Borough of Lambeth 44
    Vauxhall – Albert Embankment, Vauxhall Bridge, Vauxhall Cross ... 44
    Waterloo – The Old Vic Tunnels, Westminster Bridge 51

    Borough of Lewisham 57
    New Cross – Parkside Business Estate 57

    Borough of Newham 58
    Gallions Reach – Beckton Gas Works 58

    Borough of Southwark 62
    Canada Water – Harmsworth Quays Printing Limited 62

    Borough of Tower Hamlets 64
    Crossharbour – West Ferry Printers 64
    Westferry – Canary Riverside Health Club 66

Contents

City of London **67**
Bank – Drapers' Hall 67
Barbican – Frobisher Crescent, London Wall, Smithfield Market 70
Liverpool Street – Broadgate Tower 76
Mansion House – College of Arms 79
Tower Hill – Port of London Authority Building 83

City of Westminster **86**
Bayswater – St. Sophia's Greek Orthodox Cathedral 86
Charing Cross – Charing Cross Station, Embankment Place,
    Malaysia House, National Gallery, Reform Club 89
Edgware Road – The Water Gardens 105
Green Park – Buckingham Palace, Sotheby's 108
Oxford Circus – The Langham Hotel 114
Temple – Somerset House 116
Westminster – Palace of Westminster, Parliament Square,
    Millbank, Westminster Station, Whitehall 120
    Miscellaneous Locations **131**
        Hyde Park Corner – Les Ambassadeurs Club 131
        Leicester Square – Odeon Leicester Square 133
        River Thames 137
        Victoria – Ebury Street 147

James Bond on Location Maps **149**

Places Index **155**

Film Index **157**

Acknowledgments **159**

INTRODUCTION

'The scent and smoke and sweat of a casino are nauseating at three in the morning.'

There is no conceivable way that Ian Fleming could have known that this first line, written on the 17th February 1952, in his first James Bond book, *Casino Royale*, would lead to his fictional spy being known the world over, and that it would culminate in the longest, and most successful, film franchise in history.

In this book Bond is cold and ruthless. He drives a 1933 4.5 litre Bentley, drinks champagne and dry Martinis (shaken, not stirred), smokes Morland cigarettes and carries a .25 Beretta automatic. Not exactly the iconic image portrayed on film although the basics are all present. To date the books (twelve novels and two collections of short stories) have sold in total around one hundred million copies – not bad for an author with a literary span of just over a decade, *Casino Royale* being published on the 13th April 1953 and his last book, *Octopussy and The Living Daylights*, just ninety-four pages in length, being released on the 23rd June 1966, nearly two years after Fleming's death on the 12th August 1964. For any normal author this would have been the extent of the canon, but not for Bond, since new stories have been written by the likes of Kingsley Amis (under the pseudonym of Robert Markham), Christopher Wood, John Gardner, Raymond Benson, Sebastian Faulks and Jeffery Deaver.

The books, though, may be considered small fry compared to the film success. To date there have been twenty-three 'official' films plus the satirical spoof version of *Casino Royale* and the 1983 remake of *Thunderball* in which Sean Connery played Bond for the final time in the appropriately named *Never Say Never Again*. To complete the picture there was also a 1954 American television adaptation of *Casino Royale* called *Climax!*

Total box office sales are estimated to be in the order of nearly $5 billion (or $12 billion if inflation is taken into account) on a total budget of around $1 billion (giving a healthy return on investment). It is thought that around one in five people on Earth have seen a James Bond film. Critically, however, the films have been less successful, having won just three Academy Awards in fifty-one years – for sound effects in *Goldfinger*, for visual effects in *Thunderball*, and most recently for best original song in *Skyfall*. 'Live and Let Die', 'Nobody Does It Better' (from *The Spy Who Loved Me*) and 'For Your Eyes Only' were all nominated in that category, but Adele's was the first Bond movie song to win.

Introduction

If one takes notice of the critics then the earlier films in the series are the best, the three least satisfying being *You Only Live Twice*, *The Man With The Golden Gun* and *A View to a Kill*. A recent poll of over three thousand fans in 2012, prior to the release of *Skyfall*, concluded that the best film was *On Her Majesty's Secret Service*, closely followed by *Goldfinger* and *From Russia With Love* in that order. Looking at the highest ranking films portrayed by other actors, *The Living Daylights* came seventh, *The Spy Who Loved Me* eighth, *GoldenEye* ninth and *Casino Royale* fourth (not to be confused with the spoof version of the same title, which came last). The worst 'official' Bond film was *Die Another Day*, which was not saved even by its $142 million budget.

The most successful, financially, at least, was *Dr. No*, costing just $1.2 million and grossing nearly $60 million at the box office. George Lazenby was perhaps hard done by, since *On Her Majesty's Secret Service* had a reduced budget of $7.5 million, compared with $9.5 million for the previous film, *You Only Live Twice*, but still brought in a return of over ten fold. Likewise *Diamonds Are Forever* also had a small budget of just $7.2 million but recouped a sixteen-fold return, mainly due to the re-appearance of Sean Connery. The least successful film belongs to Roger Moore – *The Man with the Golden Gun*, which with its exotic locations cost $13 million to produce but grossed just under £100 million. The sales figures speak for themselves in that, although the critics may not be won over by James Bond, the rest of the world has always been in love with this film franchise. Indeed, *Skyfall* has broken all previous United Kingdom box office records, being the first film of any kind to take more than £100 million at the box office, while in America it was the fourth highest grossing film of 2012.

But what is it about a Bond film that makes it such a success?

To some it is the story and script, while for many it is the actual portrayal of Bond, whether your favourite be Connery, Lazenby, Moore, Dalton, Brosnan or Craig. This is closely followed in popularity by the villains – who can forget the famous dialogue exchange with Goldfinger when Bond asks, "Do you expect me to talk?" to which the former replies, "No, Mr. Bond, I expect you to die!" Then there are the cameo appearances by M and Q, with his assortment of gadgets, that are almost expected in each outing, and of course a Bond film would simply not be a Bond film without those Bond girls, not forgetting their appearance in silhouette form in the stylish titles that were first inspired by Maurice Binder. Just as much a part of each film is the pre-title sequence, which sets the pace of each film, along with the gun barrel sequence. Let us not forget the stunts and action sequences, which most films cannot begin to match. Also central to each film is the music, which seems to fit seamlessly into each new adventure.

Introduction

Finally there are those exotic locations, and magnificent larger than life sets, initially created by Ken Adam, as Bond goes around the world (and even into outer space if the end titles to *Moonraker* can be believed).

So the answer is not as simple as one might expect. To be successful, a Bond film may need only one or two of these elements, but most rely on a careful balance of them all. In just two words Bond can be considered as 'sheer escapism' for a couple of hours from the real dreary world that most of us inhabit.

It is to the last of the cited reasons, the locations, that this book is dedicated, and in this volume it is just the London locations that are considered. At first this may not seem a good starting place, since Bond works for MI6 and must spend all of his time out of the country, except when he is being briefed by M. Nothing could be further from the truth! As Bond is a quintessentially British film production for the international market it follows that quite a lot of filming takes place in the United Kingdom, and in particular London. The caption on the screen in *Octopussy* may say that we are looking at the Art Repository in St. Petersburg, but filming for the scene actually took place at the Old Royal Naval College in Greenwich (page 21). Similarly, Brent Cross has doubled for Hamburg (page 13), St. Pancras station has represented that of St. Petersburg (page 17), Stoke Newington has stood in for Cuba (page 26), and Liverpool Street posed as Shanghai (page 76) in *Skyfall*. Even London itself can be deceptive: a scene at Docklands in *The World Is Not Enough* was actually shot at Chatham (covered in Volume 2).

Finding out just what was filmed where is all part of the fun of being a location detective. If this aspect of filming interests you, then read on, but beware, for certain myths about filming will be dispelled, and in future you will not be able to look at another Bond film without wondering whether what you see on the screen is actually where the filming took place, because much of the time it isn't. I hope that you enjoy reading this book, and using it to visit some of the places listed, as much as I did researching and compiling it for you.

J. P. Sperati

9

THE ENTIRE SERIES OF *JAMES BOND ON LOCATION* IS AVAILABLE FROM ALL GOOD BOOKSHOPS OR DIRECT FROM THE PUBLISHER

JAMES BOND ON LOCATION

AN UNOFFICIAL REVIEW & GUIDE TO THE LOCATIONS USED FOR THE ENTIRE FILM SERIES FROM DR. NO TO SKYFALL

VOLUME 2: U.K. (EXCL. LONDON)

DELUXE FULL COLOUR EDITION

INDEXED & WITH LOCATION MAPS

J. P. SPERATI

WWW.JAMES-BOND-ON-LOCATION.COM
WWW.BAKER-STREET-STUDIOS.COM

James Bond in London

FOR BOND LOVERS ONLY!
www.007magazine.com
Publishing the best of Bond internationally since 1979

James Bond in London

London, on the River Thames, is the largest city, urban zone and metropolitan area in the United Kingdom, and also Europe by most criteria. It has been a major settlement for over two thousand years with a history going back to Roman times, when it was called Londinium. The City of London still retains many of its medieval boundaries, and many curious traditions. The official population of London is just over eight million persons, although if the metropolitan areas are also included this number rises to somewhere between twelve and fourteen million, or one fifth of the population of the United Kingdom.

Today London is global centre for the arts, commerce, education, entertainment, fashion, finance, healthcare, media, professional services, research and development, tourism and transport. It is hardly surprising that production crews see the city as just one big film set, and although London may appear only fleetingly as itself in the James Bond series, it actually plays a rather larger role, doubling, for example, as Shanghai in *Skyfall*, as Hamburg in *Tomorrow Never Dies*, as Cuba in *Die Another Day*, as St. Petersburg in *GoldenEye*, and so on.

In fact some fifty separate locations have been used in filming, and for the purposes of this guide they are presented alphabetically by their administrative authority (borough or city) and then by the closest railway/Underground station or town/village.

Borough of Barnet

Brent Cross - Brent Cross Shopping Centre

Barnet is one of the northern outer London boroughs, forming a boundary with the county of Hertfordshire to the north, and five other London boroughs (Harrow, Brent, Camden, Haringay and Enfield) in the other directions. It is in fact the second largest borough by population, covering an area of 33 square miles, having been formed in 1965 from parts of the counties of Middlesex and Hertfordshire. There is evidence of Roman activity in the area since the 1st century, and in 1471 the Battle of Barnet was fought just to the north of what is now Chipping Barnet. It was here that the Yorkist troops led by King Edward IV killed the rebellious 'kingmaker' Richard Neville, Earl of Warwick, along with his brother, John Neville, 1st Marquess of Montagu.

As its name suggests Brent Cross was originally the name of a crossroads, thought to be close to the current junction of the North Circular Road and the start of the M1 motorway. Before that the area had been known as Renters Farm, a name dating from 1309, and it remained farmland until a sewage works was built here in the late 19th century, along with the Hendon Greyhound Stadium, which was in operation between 1935 and 1970.

[Only at Brent Cross and on the Monopoly board can you find 'Free Parking' on such a scale in London. However, in *Tomorrow Never Dies* this is not London but the car park closest to the Kempinsky Atlantic Hotel in Hamburg]

The shopping centre was opened on the 2nd March 1976 on a virgin site of fifty-two acres running parallel to the north side of the North Circular Road and to the east of the M1 motorway. It was constructed by the Hammerson Group of Companies as the first regional shopping centre in Europe. It was initially constructed in a dumbbell shape with two large stores (John Lewis and Fenwicks) at the ends and spread over two levels, the length of the main hall being 186 metres. In its time it was seen as being quite luxurious with its marble floors and an elaborate fountain under the main dome, and coach companies ran special excursions from far and wide to visit this new shopping experience. The centre was extended and refurbished in 1995 and now has well over one hundred stores and free parking (something rare in London) for eight thousand cars.

[The fourth floor at Brent Cross multi-storey car park, remarkably devoid of any cars, looking down the main aisle where Bond fires the Stinger missiles, concealed in the sunroof, at one of Carver's cars]

Originally, parking at Brent Cross was just on open ground, but when the extension arm of additional shops and restaurants was added, running north from the middle of the complex, the remainder of the open parking was replaced with a multi-storey car park, and it is here that the James Bond enthusiast should head.

Over a three week period in June 1997 up to one hundred and fifty production crew invaded the fourth floor of the car park and used up to seventeen BMW 750iL cars (many of which were not to survive the filming intact) to shoot the car chase sequence for *Tomorrow Never Dies*, in which Bond evades Carver's henchmen by driving his 'fully loaded' car from the back seat via his Ericsson mobile telephone. The effect was achieved by having the steering wheel mounted on the back seat, so that it looked as if there was no driver present.

All did not go to plan, as on the 16th June, when three vehicles were set on fire, the amount of smoke produced was greater than expected. A member of the public called the fire brigade, who arrived promptly and evacuated the area. Fortunately the shops were not affected. The sequence was co-ordinated by veteran stunt man Vic Armstrong, and attention to detail was paramount. The car park was hung with German signs and filled with left-hand drive cars bearing German licence plates. On screen the car park does look a little smaller – not only because of the different lenses used to capture the shots in a confined space, but also due to the presence of false walls added by the production crew so that if there was a driving mishap no damage would be done. Behind one of these walls was the set armoury, under the supervision of Charlie Bodycomb. Bond was very much outgunned in this sequence, since he only carried an updated Walther P99.9mm pistol, whereas the baddies were issued with MP5K sub-machine guns, CAR15 5.56 automatics with M203 grenade launchers and 12-shot riot shotguns.

[Bond's BMW 750iL exhibiting the Stinger missiles in the sunroof]

Only the very last part of the chase sequence, when Bond drives onto the roof, was not Brent Cross, but the car park of the department store Horten at Steintorwell in Hamburg. The leap from the car park roof was done at Frogmore Studios in Hertfordshire, while the landing through the window of the Avis Rent-A-Car office was back at the Kaufhof store in Hamburg and was shot by catapulting the car from the back of a truck through a pane of glass. Another trick employed during filming was when Bond's BMW runs over metal tacks, causing all the tyres to puncture, and then magically re-inflate. This was done, quite simply, by fitting the car with lower-profile rubber on the wheels with a lever inside the car that raised the tyres up, giving the impression that they were refilling with air.

Finally the very observant will note the German license number of Bond's car is B:MT2144, which was an intentional nod to *Goldfinger* in which Bond's Aston Martin DB5 had the license plate BMT 214A.

Borough of Camden
King's Cross - St. Pancras Station

King's Cross, an area straddling the boroughs of Camden and Islington, was known for much of its modern existence as a red light district. A lot has changed, though, over the past decade, in large part thanks to the new British Library building and the adjacent St. Pancras International railway station, which is now the London terminus of Eurostar services to the Continent. Indeed, some £500 million has been spend on the regeneration of this area since 2005.

Battle Bridge was the original name, since it was where a bridge once crossed the River Fleet. However, there is no evidence of any battle at this site, though unsupported folk lore has it that this was the scene of a major conflict between the Romans and Iceni tribe led by Boudica, and it is even suggested that Boudica was killed and is buried here, at what is now the area between platforms 9 and 10 at King's Cross station (maybe the inspiration for platform 9$^{3/4}$ of the Harry Potter books) and where her ghost is sometimes reported to manifest itself. Even if this is not true, the station is certainly built on the site of a former smallpox hospital.

The current name is derived from 1830, when a monument to King George IV was built at the junction of Gray's Inn Road, Pentonville Road, and New Road (which later became Euston Road, and marked the outer boundary of London). The monument was eighteen metres high and topped by a three metre tall statue of the King. It was not popular, being described as 'a ridiculous octagonal structure crowned by an absurd statue', and was demolished in 1845. The upper part was used as a *camera obscura*, while the base in turn housed a police station and a public house. The site is now occupied by King's Cross station, one of the so called 'railway cathedrals', designed by Lewis Cubitt and opened in 1852.

Meanwhile St. Pancras railway station, built on the site of the old Agar Town slums, is a far more splendid structure. The name is that of a fourteen-year-old boy who converted to Christianity and was martyred by the Emperor Diocletian.

[The Gothic exterior and eastern clock tower of St. Pancras station, with Britannia, on top of the gable to the right of the tower, looking down on King's Cross station]

The station, was built between 1863-7, is a single shed, some two hundred and ten metres long by seventy-three metres wide and thirty metres high at its apex. It was constructed of glass and iron to the design of W. H. Barlow, and at the time was the largest single span structure of its type in the world. The station is set higher than its neighbour by some six metres due to the Regent's Canal, but the space beneath the station was not wasted, since it was always intended to be used for the storage of beer barrels from Burton-on-Trent, the iron supporting columns being spaced in measurements of beer barrels so as to maximise the available area.

Unlike King's Cross station, which has a plain front and a hotel to the side, St. Pancras station built its Midland Grand Hotel right on Euston Road. As it was to be a symbol for the importance of the Midland Railway no expense was spared. In fact, of the eleven designs submitted by various architects in 1865, that which was accepted by the company was the most expensive plan at £316,000 (though the final bill was £438,000). This was the design by George Gilbert Scott, who envisaged a high Gothic style construction consisting of pinnacles, towers and gables and, in contrast to King's Cross station, was said by the architect himself to be 'possibly too good for its purpose'. It has been said by others to be 'the finest building in London'. The structure is one hundred and seventy-two metres long, with a west tower seventy-six metres high and an east clock tower even higher at eighty-two metres. Standing on a gable beside the east tower is a bronze statue of Britannia (actually part of the lightning conductor) who is said the have her back to Euston station while looking down on King's Cross station. The hotel had two hundred and fifty bedrooms and was said to be 'the most sumptuous and best-conducted hotel in the empire'.

The hotel was ahead of its time in many respects – it was the first building in London to have a revolving door installed, and guests could listen in to theatre and concert performances through the hotel's telephone system – but it lacked other amenities, such as central heating and *en suite* bathrooms, which by the 20th century most guests considered essential. Patronage declined, and in 1935 it closed and became railway offices, changing its name to St. Pancras Chambers. The building also suffered because Scott used Edward Gripper's patent bricks, which were dressed with several different types of stone (such as red and grey Peterhead granite) which, although magnificent in looks, are porous and so weather far more quickly than the ordinary London bricks of King's Cross station. With the ever-mounting expense of upkeep, the whole building was left to slowly become a relic of a past era – sad and unsafe to enter. There were frequent calls for demolition, but when St. Pancras was announced as the new terminus for Eurostar trains a saviour was at hand. From 2003 to 2007 the whole area was redeveloped, with a large new building to the north for suburban services and the opening up of the vaults to house the new booking hall and shopping area. The former hotel has been refurbished to become once again a first class hotel with private apartments.

Films shot here include *The Ipcress File* (1965), *Brannigan* (1975), *Voyage of the Damned* (1976), *McVicar* (1980), *The Fourth Protocol* (1987), *Shirley Valentine* (1989), *King Ralph* (1991), *Shining Through* (1992), *Chaplin* (1992), *Howards End* (1992), *The Secret Garden* (1993), *102 Dalmatians* (2000), *Batman Begins* (2005), *Somers Town* (2008), *Harry Potter and the Chamber of Secrets* (2002) and *Harry Potter and the Deathly Hallows: Part 2* (2011).

[The magnificent and imposing Barlow roof as seen in 2009 after the St. Pancras station refurbishment]

As far as James Bond is concerned, platform 5 had a fleeting appearance in *GoldenEye* as the main terminus in St. Petersberg, where Natalya is seen disembarking from some old green British Railways Mark 1 carriages. St. Pancras Station was also to have been the scene of a staged train crash in *On Her Majesty's Secret Service* (page 53).

ROYAL BOROUGH OF GREENWICH

GREENWICH - OLD ROYAL NAVAL COLLEGE

The modern Borough of Greenwich to the east of the city only came into existence in 1965 when the old boundaries were extended to include most of the neighbouring borough of Woolwich, with the 'Royal' designation being granted in 2012 to mark the Diamond Jubilee of Queen Elizabeth II. The area is world famous as the traditional location of the Prime Meridian on which all Coordinated Universal Time is based – hence the designation of Greenwich Mean Time. The Royal Observatory was started in 1675 and completed the following year to the design of Sir Christopher Wren for the modest cost of £520.

[The Old Royal Naval College showing the split in the buildings so as to give an uninterrupted view from Queen's House]

In 1011-1014 the Danish fleet lay off Greenwich while the invaders camped to the east of the present borough at a location they referred to as being a 'green place on the bay' (Grenewic in Anglo-Saxon). The Domesday Book records that there was a manor here held by Bishop Odo of Bayeux, and by 1300 there was certainly a royal palace, or hunting lodge, since King Edward I is known to have made offerings at the chapel of the Virgin Mary. In 1417 the Duke of Gloucester enclosed 190 acres of land (now Greenwich Park) and built a palace called Bella Court (also known as Greenwich Palace) in 1426. This was the birthplace of many in the House of Tudor, including King Henry VIII and Queen Elizabeth I. Appropriately enough in 1605 King James II gave the park and palace to his wife, Anne of Denmark, who set about building Queen's House which was completed in 1635. At this time Greenwich became a fashionable resort with many grand houses being built.

Following the Civil War Greenwich was not sold off, as were most of the Crown lands, but designated as a home for the Protector, Oliver Cromwell. Greenwich Palace fell into disrepair, but after the Restoration King Charles II planned the construction of a new palace to the designs of John Webb (a pupil of Inigo Jones), but ran out of money in 1669 with just one wing, the King Charles Building, completed. It was not until 1692 that Queen Mary decided that the project should be completed in order to provide a hospital for disabled seamen, corresponding to the recently finished Chelsea Hospital. The buildings were designed by Sir Christopher Wren (who gave his time free of charge) along with his assistant Nicholas Hawksmoor.

[Part of the undercroft of the King William Building under the Painted Hall where M is seen with the Union flag covered coffins of MI6 personnel in *Skyfall*]

Wren demolished all that remained of the original palace save for the undercroft that is now the basement of the Queen Anne Building, which was completed in 1728. However, there was controversy as Wren's plans would have obscured the view from Queen's House, and so Queen Mary ordered that the new buildings should be split in two so that the house should remain visible from the waterfront. Dr. Samuel Johnson, who lived in Greenwich when he first came to London, remarked "that the parts were too much detached to make one great whole".

Vanburgh succeeded Wren and completed the King William Building in 1705, but did not finish the façade of the west front for another twenty-one years. He also built two houses for himself in the area, Vanburgh Castle (in the style of a fortress and said to be England's first folly) and Ranger's House. In 1708 James Thornhill (who also painted the interior of the dome of St. Paul's Cathedral) began work on the Painted Hall. In the central section of the ceiling of the lower hall he depicted William and Mary dispensing Peace and Liberty to a grateful Europe, and in the upper hall we see Queen Anne and her husband acknowledging the salutation of Victory. For nineteen years' work, Thornhill, who was knighted in 1720, received £3 per square yard for the ceiling and just £1 per square yard for the walls. In January 1806 Lord Nelson's body lay in state here for three days, and more than thirty thousand people came to pay their respects.

The buildings were really too grand for a hospital, as Dr Johnson recognised. In 1771 a Captain Baillie complained that "Columns, colonnades and friezes ill accord with bully beef and sour beer mixed with water." The administrators of the hospital were accused of cruelty and corruption, and the number of pensioners declined so sharply that in 1869 the buildings were vacated.

Four years later the Royal Naval College moved here from Portsmouth, remaining at Greenwich until the site was taken over by the University of Greenwich in 1996. The following year the entire complex, including the Queen's House, the Royal Observatory and Greenwich Park, was designated a UNESCO World Heritage site, and in 2001 Trinity College of Music moved into the King Charles Court. There are other reminders of Britain's maritime past, for just behind the Old Royal Naval College is the National Maritime Museum, comprising two-and-a-half million items housed in sixteen galleries and covering every aspect of Britain's seafaring heritage, while close by in King William Walk lies the most famous tea clipper, the Cutty Sark, which was built in 1869 and was still carrying cargoes when she was bought and restored in 1922.

It will come as no surprise that Greenwich has been seen in around fifty film and television productions, the most notable of which are: *Charge of the Light Brigade* (1968), *Anne of the Thousand Days* (1969), *Murder by Decree* (1979), *The Bounty* (1984), *Patriot Games* (1992), *Four Weddings and a Funeral* (1994), *Sense and Sensibility* (1995), *Lara Croft: Tomb Raider* (2001), *The Mummy Returns* (2001), *What a Girl Wants* (2003), *The Madness of King George* (1994), *Vanity Fair* (2004), *Amazing Grace*

(2006), *The Golden Compass* (2007), *The Oxford Murders* (2008), *Dorian Gray* (2009), *Sherlock Holmes* (2009), *The King's Speech* (2010), *Gulliver's Travels* (2010), *The Wolfman* (2010), *Sherlock Holmes: A Game of Shadows* (2011), *Pirates of the Caribbean: On Stranger Tides* (2011), *The Iron Lady* (2011), *Les Miserables* (2012) and *Thor: The Dark World* (2013).

Two James Bond films have used the Old Royal Naval College in their productions, albeit only for a few seconds in each case. In *Octopussy* a side door in the Queen Mary Building became the entrance to the Art Repository in St. Petersberg, through which General Orlov enters to discover that the reproduction Fabergé egg has been stolen in transit. The building, complete with Russian guards, is convincing apart from the landmark chimneys of Greenwich power station in the background.

Most recently in *Skyfall* it is in the undercroft of the same building that M is seen inspecting the coffins of personnel following the attack on the MI6 offices at Vauxhall Cross. The original scene was longer but was trimmed in the final edit.

[The same camera angle as used in *Octopussy* with the repository door just visible on the left]

Entry to the Chapel, the Painted Hall and the Visitor Centre is free, though the Painted Hall and the Chapel may be closed at short notice for maintenance or for private functions, so do check the official website (www.ornc.org).

NORTH GREENWICH - THE O2

The O2, formerly the Millennium Dome, has a rather chequered history. The structure is essentially a large white canopy that encloses about 20 acres of land on the site of a former gasworks at the tip of the Greenwich peninsula, on the south side of the River Thames. The canopy is suspended from twelve hundred-metre-high steel masts by forty-five miles of steel cable, and is reckoned to be the largest domed structure in the world, being three hundred and sixty-five metres in diameter and fifty-two metres high at the centre. It is constructed of PTFE, a durable and weather-resistant glass fibre fabric, but with an estimated lifespan of only twenty-five years. The building was conceived in 1994 as a flagship project for the Millennium, in the tradition of the Great Exhibition and the Festival of Britain. Having failed to attract enough private investment, construction finally began in 1997, funded by the National Lottery. The architect was Richard Rogers.

The O2 with no sign of James Bond clinging to the canopy as he did in *The World Is Not Enough*]

The Millennium Dome opened on New Year's Eve 1999, with a New Millennium Spectacular attended by members of the Royal Family. There followed the year-long Millennium Experience, featuring fourteen zones (Body, Mind, Faith, Work, Play and so on) along with other attractions. Despite criticisms that it was lacking in content, more than six million people visited the Millennium Experience, but that was not enough to produce an operating profit. National Audit Office figures showed that the total cost at the liquidation of the New Millennium Experience Company in 2002 was £789 million, of which less than £200 million was covered by ticket sales.

For several years the site remained closed, except for some special one-off uses, such as at Christmas 2004, when it became a shelter for the homeless. On the 31st May 2005, the Millennium Dome officially became The O2, in a £6 million deal with the telecommunications company of that name. At the same time, the new owners, the Anschultz Entertainment Group, began a redevelopment of the site, which, over the next few years, saw the 150-acre site transformed. Within the dome they installed a 23,000-seat indoor arena, a 2,200-seat music club, a cinema, exhibition space, bars and restaurants, while the waterfront area gained office accommodation, ten thousand new homes, a school, a hotel, and new transport links. The new complex, costing £600 million, was opened to the public on the 24th June 2007. The latest spectacular addition is the Emirates Air Line cable car that crosses the Thames at a height of ninety metres (nearly three hundred feet). It began operating in June 2012.

It was in 1999 that James Bond was seen clinging to the O2 canopy at the end of the pre-title chase sequence of *The World Is Not Enough*. A detailed description of the boat chase locations is given on pages 137-147.

BOROUGH OF HACKNEY

STOKE NEWINGTON - KINGSLAND HOUSE

Hackney, located immediately to the northeast of the City of London, includes the areas of Shoreditch, Hoxton and Stoke Newington. In the middle ages, the main landowner here was the Order of St. John of Jerusalem. The oldest building in the borough, dating back to the 13th century, is St. Augustine's Tower, all that survives of the old parish church, founded by the Knights of St. John. The village of Hackney flourished from the Tudor to the late Georgian periods as a rural retreat, but this ended with the coming of the railway in the 1850s. Later, a familiar figure in the area was Alfred Hitchcock, who made many of his early films at Gainsborough Studios, located in Poole Street, Hoxton.

Stoke Newington, meaning 'new town in the wood', was originally a Saxon settlement built along Ermine Street, the Roman road between London and York. However, there is evidence of earlier habitation from Palaeolithic remains found near to Hackney Brook. In the 17th century it was a place for dissenters, banned from living in the City of London, which accounts for the numerous Nonconformist chapels and meeting houses in the area. Daniel Defoe was perhaps the most famous inhabitant at this time. The 18th century brought with it the building of many grand houses in red brick. Thomas Cubitt was one of the best known developers, prior to his more illustrious projects in Belgravia and Pimlico.

In the 19th century the population was increased by the arrival of many Jewish refugees. By the late 20th century the immigrants came mainly from the Caribbean, south Asia, Cyprus, Turkey, Afghanistan, Kurdistan and the Balkans. Author Iain Sinclair commented that Stoke Newington is 'the perfect place in which to stay lost: limboland, London's inter-zone. Large shabby properties that ask no questions. Internal exile with a phoney rent-book'.

[Kingsland House is not immediately associated with Cuba]

Heading north along the main Stoke Newington Road (the A10), on the right hand side we see Kingsland House. A more unlikely location to stand in for Cuba one cannot imagine. However, that is exactly what the building became for a few days during filming of *Die Another Day*, when Kingsland House became the interior of the Cuban cigar factory that Bond visits. A closer look will reveal that this is an iconic building with an imposing temple-like shop front combined with original and beautiful Art Deco mosaic interiors. In 1929 the building housed the country's largest suit factory for the reputable tailoring brand of Daks. After they moved out it became a Turkish community centre and market. Since 2011 it has been part of the Beyond Retro chain of specialist clothing shops, dealing with handpicked vintage garments for sale to style-conscious shoppers.

BOROUGH OF HILLINGDON

HAREFIELD - SUMMERHOUSE LANE

The borough of Hillingdon is the most westerly outer borough of London, incorporating areas that were once part of Middlesex. It is home to Heathrow Airport and Brunel University, and is the second largest London borough by area. The south of the borough tends to be given over to industry whereas the north is in the main residential, having been expanded with the extension of the Metropolitan Railway from Harrow on the Hill to Uxbridge in the early 1900s, and the gradual establishment of stops along the line – the birth of what became known as Metro-land.

[The location, filmed at night, where the Mercedes pursuing Bond in *Goldfinger* explodes as it traverses down the cliff]

Harefield is about as far as one can go from Charing Cross without leaving Greater London. The village was listed in the Domesday Book as Herefelle, meaning open land used by an army. The name is unconnected with the fact that from the 12th century the moorland nearby was owned by the Knights of St. John of Jerusalem. Part of the nave of St. Mary's church dates from the same period. By 1446 both Harefield and neighbouring Moorhall were the property of the Newdigate family, remaining in their possession until the 1920s. Among the Newdigate tombs in the parish church are two carved by Grinling Gibbons. However, the area changed in the late 18th century with the arrival of the Grand Union Canal (to the west) along with lime kilns and copper mills. After World War II surviving mansions were given over to official use, with Harefield Park becoming the staff quarters for Harefield Hospital (now famous for its pioneering heart surgery and transplants but originally a sanatorium in the 1930s). Harefield would seem to be the place for heroes since the village can boast no fewer than three recipients of the Victoria Cross, from the Crimean War and World War I.

Proceeding west from the village along the main Park Lane, just before you reach the Grand Union Canal, there is a turning on the right to Summerhouse Lane, which runs parallel to the canal. If you go up here, past the Coppermill Lock to the very end of the road you reach a small light industrial estate called Coppermill Business Park. It is from the car park behind the main building that you will find the small chalk cliff that in *Goldfinger* was the setting for the scene in which the Mercedes chasing Bond is caught out by the oil slick from the modified Aston Martin DB5 and skids off the road (actually Burnham Beeches covered in Volume 2), explodes into a ball of flames as it goes down the cliff, and finally lands back at Pinewood Studios (also covered Volume 2).

RUISLIP GARDENS - R.A.F. NORTHOLT

In the north-west part of the borough of Ealing is Northolt, known for most of its existence as Northall, which until the 1920s was just agricultural land. The aerodrome, although only a mile or so to the west, is in fact entirely within the neighbouring borough of Hillingdon, with the closest station being two stops away at Ruislip Gardens on the Central Line. It was opened in 1915, having been built for the Royal Flying Corps, who flew BE2c aircraft patrols against Zeppelin raids over London.

The Officers' Mess, built around 1920, is still operational, as is one hangar and several barrack blocks dating from that period. In the 1930s, R.A.F. Northolt was the first station to operate the Hawker Hurricane and during World War II was again one of the key airfields in the defence of London. During the Battle of Britain, Northolt was home to a series of allied and British Hurricane and Spitfire squadrons, including a complete Polish wing (number 303 Polish Squadron having the honour of clocking up more kills than any other squadron during the Battle of Britain).

[A private jet takes off from the single 1,684 metre long runway at R.A.F. Northolt in west London, but unlike Bond's aircraft in *Goldfinger* it is not bound for lunch at the White House]

In 1946 the airfield was used for civil flights whilst Heathrow Airport was under construction, and by 1952 Northolt was the busiest airfield in Europe, handling an annual total of fifty thousand air movements.

More recently the station has become the hub of military flying operations in the London area. Northolt has been extensively redeveloped since 2006 to accommodate these changes, becoming home to the British Forces Post Office, which moved to a newly constructed headquarters and sorting office on the site. Units currently based at R.A.F. Northolt include No. 32 (The Royal) Squadron, the Queen's Colour Squadron, 600 (City of London) Squadron, No. 1 Aeronautical Information Documents Unit, the Central Band of the R.A.F. and the Air Historical Branch. In late 2011 it was announced that R.A.F. Northolt would be the forward base for Typhoon fast jets and the base for air security for the 2012 London Olympic Games.

No doubt due to its proximity to London, the airfield has been used in a number of television productions including *The Winds of War*, *The Bill*, *Waking the Dead*, *Doctor Who*, *Red Dwarf* and *Ashes to Ashes*.

[Hangar 5 looking much the same as it did in 1963 when scenes from *Goldfinger* was filmed here]

Hangar 5 was used in the final scenes of *Goldfinger*, standing in for Kentucky Airport from where Bond leaves for his lunch date at the White House with the President, and also where the actual pilots are later found just inside the hangar doors (having been bound and stripped by Goldfinger, who has hijacked their aircraft, along with Pussy Galore at the controls). The old control tower from which Felix Leiter watches the radar image of the subsequent aircraft crash has long since been demolished.

Earlier in the same film Hangar 311 is seen with a large banner reading 'Pussy Galore's Flying Circus' hung over the front. It is clearly in shot when Pussy Galore's female pilots land, and are seen running towards their leader to report the success of their final practice run over Fort Knox.

The production crew returned the following year for *Thunderball*, as the main gate was used as the entrance to the unknown airbase where Angelo, posing as Major Derval, arrives, showing his identification prior to his briefing and flight in the nuclear-armed Vulcan aircraft that he subsequently steals for SPECTRE.

James Bond in London

[The R.A.F. Northolt war memorial just inside the main entrance]

The most famous scene filmed here was the one for *Octopussy*, in which Hangar 311 is seen to be blown up (with the help of miniatures). In the pre-title sequence, Bond arrives at a gymkhana, driving a Range Rover that's pulling a horse-trailer, inside which is the Acrostar BD-5J Jet. The action supposedly takes place in an unnamed South American country, where the uniforms resemble those worn in Cuba, but it was filmed on land between Hangar 311 and Crash Gate 1, which was dressed with a few palm trees. Bond, in the guise of Colonel Toro, infiltrates the adjacent air base and gains access to the hangar, where he places a bomb in the nose cone of a fighter equipped with a prototype radar device. Unfortunately he is apprehended by the real Colonel Toro, and the bomb is defused.

Naturally Bond manages to complete his mission. He escapes in the Acrostar, evading some Rapier surface-to-air missiles, and guiding one of them into the hangar, where it explodes, while Bond flies free. Just before he runs out of fuel, he does a victory roll and then brings his aircraft down at a filling station, conveniently sited across the border, where he asks the attendant to "fill her up, please!"

[A tight fit for Roger Moore as he is propelled through Hangar 311]

The shot in which the hangar is destroyed did present some problems for the film crew, since although it was feasible to fly the Acrostar through the hangar it would take rather less than a second, and would not make for a good film sequence. Acclaimed stunt pilots Corkey Fornof and Rick Holley did all the actual flying (which was in fact filmed in Utah) while Roger Moore was in the cockpit as the aircraft appeared to fly on its side through the hangar. It was the idea of the special effects co-ordinator, John Richardson, to attach the Acrostar to a pole that was mounted onto the roof of an old Jaguar XJ-6, which was then driven through the hangar at seventy-five miles per hour. The shot required scores of soldiers (some actually from R.A.F. Northolt) to be in the foreground to hide the car. In fact all did not go to plan, as the Jaguar's throttle jammed just as it was exiting the hangar, throwing the car into several 360-degree spins and coming to a halt just a few metres away from a very expensive operational helicopter parked nearby. The remainder of the effect of the Acrostar entering and leaving the hangar was done using miniatures, so the audience see the aeroplane fly into the background between a foreground miniature and the real hangar, and of course it was a miniature that was blown up, not the real hangar. Some of the background shots were also done at R.A.F. Oakley (see Volume 2).

Finally, along the northern perimeter of the base is Crash Gate 1, an emergency access point to the outside world, close to where filming took place for *The World Is Not Enough*. The scene is the one in which Bond, having dispatched Davidoff, swaps identities and boards the Antonov aeroplane bound for the nuclear facility in Kazakhstan.

BOROUGH OF HOUNSLOW

FELTHAM - BEDFONT LAKES OFFICE PARK

[Back of one of the IBM buildings at Bedfont Lakes. This became the headquarters of the Carver Media Group Network in *Tomorrow Never Dies*]

Apart from the town of the same name, the largest settlements in this outer western borough are Chiswick, Brentford and Feltham. There are records of Hounslow, meaning 'Hund's mound' (possible his burial place), as early as the 13th century. Later it became the first stop on the important coach route from London to Southampton, Bath, Bristol and Exeter, and consequently many inns were built along the Great West Road (now the main A30). In the latter half of the 20th century the area grew rapidly due to the expansion of Heathrow Airport close by. The borough was also known for the many famous global manufacturers, such as Firestone, Gillette and Coty who made their headquarters along what became known as the Golden Mile.

Feltham itself, meaning a 'home in a field', originally an Anglo-Saxon settlement, was almost totally destroyed by fire in 1634. It was rebuilt soon afterwards, together with the manor house, which was demolished as recently as 1966. The main economic activity of the area was market gardening, a popular variety of pea, the Feltham First, being grown here. In time the market gardens were replaced with light industry (including the manufacture of trams), gravel and aggregate extraction.

Some of the former gravel pits now form Bedfont Lakes Country Park, which extends to over 180-acres. It was opened in 1995 and is currently being developed as a water-focussed nature reserve. Within this country park is the office park, which has become the home to a number of national, and international, companies such as IBM, SAP and Cisco, Home Office, Lindt Chocolates, Birds Eye and Stratus Technology. It aims to provide an unspoilt working environment with recreational activities, with the convenience of being close to Heathrow Airport.

[New Square where Bond arrives for Carver's media party in his BMW, hired from the Avis Rent-A-Car desk at Hamburg Airport earlier in the day]

It is no wonder then that this peaceful location was chosen for the headquarters of the Carver Media Group Network, not Hamburg as *Tomorrow Never Dies* would have the audience believe. This is where

Bond attends the media reception and meets up with his old love, Paris Carver. The filming took place in New Square, where Bond is seen arriving and having his 'fully loaded' BMW valet parked, and in the atrium of the main IBM building, which today serves as the staff canteen.

ROYAL BOROUGH OF KENSINGTON & CHELSEA

FULHAM BROADWAY - BROMPTON CEMETERY CHAPEL

After the City of Westminster, Kensington & Chelsea is the wealthiest, and most densely populated, borough in England. The borough is home to a number of landmark facilities, such as major museums at South Kensington, universities, embassies, department stores such as Harrods, as well as the world famous Notting Hill Carnival.

Originally an Anglo-Saxon settlement, from Norman times until the early 16th century Kensington was owned by the Earls of Oxford. The area was largely rural, the southern part being famous for its nurseries and market gardens, which survived until the 19th century, when house-building became more profitable. The north of Kensington was mainly given over to arable farming until the 17th, century when a number of large mansions were built. Among these were Holland House, Campden House and Nottingham House, which later became Kensington Palace. In 1705 John Bowack described Kensington as having 'ever been resorted to by persons of quality ... and is inhabited by gentry and persons of note', something which has changed little since. The title of 'Royal' was actually conferred on the borough of Kensington (before its merger with Chelsea in 1965) to mark the birthplace of Queen Victoria.

The origins of Chelsea are open to debate, with spellings such as Chelcheya, Chelched and Chelchythe being among many that appear on old documents. Certainly there is a record of Offa, King of the Mercians, holding a Synod here in 787. Sir Thomas More lived here in 1520 when it was known locally as 'the village of palaces' as King Henry VIII, the Duke of Norfolk and the Earl of Shewsbury all had residences in the area. The most famous building, though, is the Chelsea Hospital, begun by Sir Christopher Wren in 1682 as a home for old soldiers. The area also became known for its writers and artists, Swift, Addison, Carlyle, Leigh Hunt, Whistler and Rossetti all being associated with Chelsea. In the 1960s and

1970s the King's Road was known as a centre of fashion, with Mary Quant and Vivienne Westwood having shops here. Other important features of the borough have included the Chelsea Physic garden, the Chelsea Porcelain Works and more recently Chelsea Football Club.

[Brompton Cemetery became the setting in *GoldenEye* for the church of Our Lady of Smolensky in St. Petersburg]

The Brompton Cemetery in Old Brompton Road was started by the West of London and Westminster Cemetery Company, who bought 40-acres of land from Lord Kensington in 1837. The land was not consecrated until 1840, and meanwhile a competition was held to decide the best design. The winner was Benjamin Baud, who envisaged ornate walls, chapels, catacombs and buildings. It was to be a formal affair with a wide main avenue leading from the entrance to a domed octagonal chapel from which long arms of catacombs would reach out to form a 'Great Circle', on each side of which was to be a further chapel. The central building was to be Anglican with the outer chapels for Roman Catholics and Dissenters respectively.

Unfortunately the company ran almost immediately into financial trouble, and only the octagonal central chapel was completed to plan. The catacombs, although they do form a circle, were never fully finished to Baud's design. However, some catacombs were constructed along the western wall. Baud had trouble getting paid for work already done, and had to endure protracted haggling over the costs. In 1852 the cemetery was purchased by the General Board of Health, thus becoming the first burial ground under state control. Very soon it was full, and now boasts upwards of thirty-five thousand monuments, including many to famous persons such as the author George Borrow, the composer Constant Lambert, the actor Brian Glover and the suffragette leader Emmeline Pankhurst.

The Anglican octagonal chapel, which was based upon St. Peter's Basilica in Rome, became the exterior of the church of Our Lady of Smolensky in St. Petersburg, where Natalya goes to meet her 'friend' Boris in *GoldenEye*. The interior shots, though, were done at the St. Sophia Greek Cathedral in Bayswater (page 86).

IMPERIAL WHARF - SNAKE RANCH STUDIOS

Close to Imperial Wharf station, and dominating the area with its two chimneys, is the disused Lots Road Power Station. Lots Road itself is named after the lots of ground which originally belonged to Chelsea Manor and over which the parishioners had rights to graze their animals at certain times of the year. It was a notoriously rough area for most of its existence. The power station was built between 1902 and 1905, specifically to provide electricity to the District Line. Still in service in 1990, it was at that time providing around two-thirds of the entire electricity needs of London Transport. There were ambitious plans to re-equip the plant to become a high-efficiency gas station that would have produced a surplus of energy which could then be sold into the national grid. However, nothing came of this proposal, and the site closed in 2002. Planning permission has been granted for conversion into shops, restaurants and flats, and for the construction of additional buildings, but work has been indefinitely delayed.

Set back from the main road, the Snake Ranch Studios actually consisted of a very basic rehearsal room, and from the mid-1980s a recording studio, located at No. 90 Lots Road. They were owned jointly by composer/musicians Richard Harvey and Nick Glennie-Smith who used them as a vehicle for projects concerning their folk-rock band, *Griffin*, but also a place in which to develop their work in film, television and library music. The main studio could accommodate up to twenty-five musicians, and among the recordings made there were the soundtracks for *The Last Emperor* (1987), *Rosencrantz & Guildenstern Are Dead* (1990), *Gregory's Two Girls* (1999), *The Honorary Consul* (1983) and *Flyfishing* (2002). The studios closed in 2004 but the entrance through which Bond and Wade drive in the blue Trabant in *GoldenEye* to visit Valentine Zukowski is still recognisable, especially since the deserted Lots Road Power Station is clearly visible in the background.

[The site of the former Snake Ranch Studios at No. 90 Lots Road, with the entrance to the 606 Club, a possible inspiration for Zukowski's night club, on the left]

It will be recalled that in the film Zukowski is based in a night club. The use of this location was entirely appropriate as the Trabant emerges from the right hand side of the picture from outside the entrance to the 606 Club, a famous London night club for jazz lovers, which has been situated in the basement of No. 90 Lots Road since May 1988. The quality of singing, though, is much higher than that of Zukowski's mistress, Irina, the 'very talented girl' singing *Stand By Your Man*, who is told to 'take a hike' after Bond enquires as to 'who's strangling the cat'.

SLOANE SQUARE - CADOGAN SQUARE

[In *Skyfall* it seems that M has moved from Canary Wharf to John Barry's flat in Cadogan Square]

Sloane Square is named after Sir Hans Sloane who was at one time lord of the Manor of Chelsea. In 1771 the grassland was enclosed and cobbled, with houses being built around the square some years later. The Underground railway station was opened in 1868, but not without some difficulty since the River Westbourne runs across the station, and still does today, being carried over the tracks in a large iron pipe. The station suffered a direct hit from a bomb during World War II, with many casualties from the two trains that happened to be standing in the station at the time. The station restoration took eleven years to complete, re-opening in 1951 in time for the Festival of Britain. The two most prominent buildings around the square are Peter Jones, a department store originally opened by a young Welsh draper's assistant in 1877, and the Royal Court Theatre. In the centre of the square is a fountain, by the sculptor Gilbert Ledward, which was unveiled in 1951. It consists of a kneeling bronze figure of Venus, holding a vase and pouring water from a conch shell. The basin is decorated with a relief depicting Charles II and Nell Gwynn seated by the River Thames.

North of the square, on the left hand side of Sloane Street, is Cadogan Gate leading to Cadogan Square. This is part of the estate named after Charles Cadogan, who in 1717 married Elizabeth, the younger daughter of Sir Hans Sloane. On the latter's death Lord Cadogan, as he was by now, also became lord of the Manor of Chelsea and a major landowner in the area.

Cadogan Square was a major 19th century development and one of the first to favour red brick over stucco, under the watchful eye of Colonel W. T. Makins, chairman of the Cadogan and Hans Place Estate Limited, a development company formed in 1875. The company actually sublet most of the land to other building contractors, letting them take most of the financial risks. The north and east sides of the square were designed by G. T. Robinson for Trollope and Sons. The south side is the work of J. J. Stevenson, and in the south-west corner are three houses by Norman Shaw. All these, and the houses by A. J. Adams, H. A. Peto and Ernest George, are in the so-called Queen Anne style, in contrast to the Gothic house in the north-east corner, designed by G. E. Street for the daughters of the Bishop of Gloucester.

Among the square's many distinguished residents was John Barry at No. 82. As composer of soundtracks for no fewer than eleven of the James Bond films between 1963 and 1987, as well as winner of five Oscars, Barry needs no introduction. He died in January 2011, his three-bedroom flat remaining empty, and available for rent at around £16,000 per month. The Bond producers have always been fond of the odd homage to Ian Fleming and others associated with Bond, such as when John Barry made a cameo appearance conducting the orchestra at the end of *The Living Daylights* (for which he wrote what would become his final Bond score). Barbara Broccoli, the James Bond producer, and John Barry were close friends in real life, so it was no accident that in February 2012 the *Skyfall* production team descended on John Barry's old flat to film the sequence in which Bond, having seemingly returned from the dead, confronts M at home. This is a change from *Casino Royale* in which the viewer sees M in a very modern apartment in Canary Wharf.

MISCELLANEOUS LOCATIONS

SLOANE SQUARE - WELLINGTON SQUARE HENNIKER MEWS

It is not a film location, but we should mention that Commander Bond actually lived in this area, in a 'comfortable flat in a plane tree'd square off the King's Road' with a 'long big-windowed sitting room', according to *From Russia with Love*. In *Moonraker* we read that it was in a 'converted Regency house' in a 'little square', and the front door was above street level, since in *On Her Majesty's Secret Service* 'Bond went up the steps and rang two shorts and a long on the bell'.

[No. 30 Wellington Square]

Bond also wonders if the flat will be too small for him and Tracy (let alone all the children she wants them both to have!).

There are several squares off King's Road, which runs west from Sloane Square, though some such as Markham Square and Royal Avenue are too large. The favoured address by most scholars is Wellington Square, and according to John Pearson at *The Sunday Times* No. 30 is the most likely candidate. However, it should be considered that, as with Conan Doyle and Sherlock Holmes's residence in Baker Street, Ian Fleming probably had no fixed address in mind.

[One of the many mews located in the Sloane Square area]

[David Richards, the chairman of Aston Martin Lagonda (right), shakes hands with Roger Carey, the chairman of the Aston Martin Heritage Trust, at the plaque unveiling on the 15th January 2013, with 'A3', the oldest surviving Aston Martin, and a 2013 Centenary Edition Vanquish also in attendance]

On screen the viewer only once gets to see the outside of Bond's home in *Live and Let Die* as M, along with Moneypenny, visits at the beginning of the film in order to brief and equip Bond, now in the shape of Roger Moore, for his next assignment to New York. Unfortunately this was not a location shoot but a studio set, the creation of production designer Syd Cain, who envisaged Bond in a mews property. This is not too far-fetched since the whole area is dotted with such mews.

Finally in this section, a little further along King's Road, heading west and then north into Beaufort Street, left into Elms Park Road and right into Callow Street we reach Henniker Mews (actually slightly closer to either Gloucester Road or South Kensington Underground stations) where the properties again resemble the set design from *Live and Let Die*.

However, the real reason for its inclusion here is a green plaque, unveiled on the 15th January 2013 to commemorate the centenary of the incorporation of Bamford & Martin Limited, who were located at No. 16 Henniker Mews. Formerly it was the depot of Hesse and Savory but became occupied by Lionel Martin and Robert Bamford in late 1912. It was here they began construction on a very unique motorcar known as 'Coal Scuttle', which was in fact the very first Aston Martin vehicle. Not long after World War I had started, the small factory closed, with both owners joining the war effort, but for those who are fans of the marque this is the birthplace of Aston Martin and well worth the walk if in the area.

BOROUGH OF LAMBETH

VAUXHALL - ALBERT EMBANKMENT
VAUXHALL BRIDGE
VAUXHALL CROSS

The modern borough of Lambeth, situated to the south of the River Thames and extending from Hungerford railway bridge to Vauxhall, was until the 18th century mostly marshland and a favoured area for duck shooting. Apart from Lambeth Palace, the official residence of the Archbishop of Canterbury, built in 1495, nothing survives from this era. Interestingly, the area, and in particular the wells at Lambeth Walk, were famous in their time for their medicinal waters. Today the place is just part of the sprawling metropolis, with its fair share of industry and open spaces, along with housing ranging from slums and high-rise flats to rather grander buildings. Lambeth has the highest population density in London, high unemployment and the largest number of homicides of any London borough. The stretch along the River Thames, though, is a tourist district and quite safe to visit.

[The Albert Embankment as viewed from Millbank using the same camera angle as in Dr. No]

Lambeth Palace was built almost opposite the Palace of Westminster, necessitating a link between the two in the form of a horse ferry (which was certainly in operation in 1513). This was one of the few places on the River Thames where a coach and horses could cross. It was not without problems; in 1633 the ferry sank under the weight of Archbishop Laud's belongings while he was moving into Lambeth Palace, and in 1656 Oliver Cromwell's coach also sank here.

Lambeth Bridge is the location in *Harry Potter and the Prisoner of Azkaban* where the Knight Bus has to shrink in width and pass in between two Volvo Super Olympian double-decker buses. Another (equally improbable) bus chase occurs close to here in Lambeth Palace Road, which runs from Lambeth Bridge towards St. Thomas' Hospital, in *The Mummy Returns* (2001). The road can again be seen in *School for Scoundrels* (1960) as it is where Ian Carmichael runs after a bus, only to fall off and meet Janette Scott, with whom he falls in love, and *Genevieve* (1953) in which Kenneth More drives his Spyker car into a fruit stall at the very end of the film. Meanwhile, filming outside Lambeth Palace has taken place for *Too Hot to Handle* (1960), *Blood Diamond* (2006) and *Match Point* (2005). However, for the James Bond enthusiast it is going in the other direction from Lambeth Palace along Albert Embankment towards Vauxhall that is of most interest.

[The MI6 communications centre from *Dr. No*?]

This is a broad road, around a mile in length, built by Sir Joseph Bazalgette between 1866 and 1870. In fact it was built from land reclaimed from the River Thames, hence its high cost of construction at just over £1 million. Today the road has both commercial and residential buildings in a complete mixture of architectures. Opposite Lambeth Palace itself is the curvaceous, highly glazed Parliament View building dating from 2001 and comprising nearly two hundred prestigious apartments, while adjacent is the red-brick Westminster Tower office block from 1983. A little further along is No. 8, the art deco Hampton House, designed by E. P. Wheeler, and opened by King George V in 1937 as the headquarters of the London Fire Brigade. This is not to be confused with No. 20, a 1960s office block, also called Hampton House, where the London Fire Brigade also had offices until its closure recently.

[The proposed development for Hampton House as designed by Foster + Partners. Immediately to the left of the towers is Queensborough House also seen in *Dr. No*]

The latter is the building, along with the then adjoining office block, Queensborough House, shown in *Dr. No*. Queensborough House was demolished and replaced by the Riverbank Plaza Hotel, which opened in 2005, although on council records it is still officially Queensborough House at No. 12-18 Albert Embankment. Hampton House is also due for redevelopment, and will become a series of luxurious one, two and three-bedroom apartments and penthouses in two towers. In the film the shot is so brief it is hard to tell which of the two buildings is meant to be the communications centre for MI6, where British agents from around the world report each day, and where it is discovered that Jamaica has broken off during mid-transmission.

Vauxhall takes its name from Falkes de Breauté, who built a house here in the reign of King John. Several variations of the name are recorded, including Fulke's Hall, Faukeshall and Foxhall. In the 1660s the diplomat, mathematician and inventor Sir Samuel Morland lived at Vauxhall. His house was later used as a distillery, which was still operating in 1790. Vauxhall remained a village until the 19th century, when it was swallowed up by the expanding development of Lambeth.

Today it is not an attractive area, being dominated by the SIS building downstream of Vauxhall Bridge, and the much larger (and uglier) complex of luxury apartments and office space, St. George Wharf, upstream, which dates from 2006. In the middle is the tangled confusion of the traffic interchange, Vauxhall Cross (for which there never was an Underground station despite the allusion to one in *Die Another Day*, page 54), which in 2005 was calmed somewhat by a remodelled road layout, along with the construction of a new £4 million bus station designed by Arup Associates.

[Vauxhall Bridge with the SIS Building behind]

Also squeezed in the middle, and at the westernmost end of Albert Embankment, is Vauxhall Bridge, linking Lambeth with Pimlico. The bridge, started in 1811 by Rennie was intended to be of standard masonry construction, but two years into the project the Vauxhall Bridge Company decided to adopt James Walker's cheaper cast-iron design. Originally called the Regent's Bridge, it was opened in 1816 and was the first iron bridge over the River Thames in London. In 1881 the two central piers were removed, converting three of its nine arches into one, to aid navigation. Between 1895 and 1906 the structure was replaced with the current bridge to the design of Sir Alexander Binnie, comprising five steel arches on granite piers. Pomeroy and Alfred Drury were responsible for the bronze figures of heroic size representing Pottery, Engineering, Architecture and Agriculture on the western side, with Science, Fine Arts, Local Government and Education on the other. It was a toll bridge up until 1879.

[Dame Judi Dench on Lambeth Bridge during filming of *Skyfall* in 2012 (left)]

In *Skyfall* M is seen, following her meeting with Gareth Mallory, the Intelligence and Security Committee chairman, being driven in her black Jaguar along Millbank, where she receives a taunting message via her laptop, and onto Lambeth Bridge, where her car is stopped by police moments before a bomb explodes in her office at the SIS building.

[The SIS Building at Vauxhall Cross, with a yellow London Duck Tours vehicle emerging from the river to the left of the picture]

No. 854 Albert Embankment is the official address of the SIS (Secret Intelligence Service), more commonly known as MI6. Those who work there refer to the building as Legoland, or (because it vaguely resembles an ancient Babylonia ziggurat) Babylon-on-Thames. It was built by John Laing to a design by Terry Farrell, on what was until the 1850s Vauxhall Pleasure Gardens, after which the site housed various industrial units, including a gin distillery. Interestingly when the architects were designing the complex in the 1980s, first as a urban village and then as offices, they were not told which agency would be occupying the site, since at that time the British Government did not admit to the existence of MI6.

A press release by the landowners in February 1989 stated that the building (yet to be started) had been sold for £130 million with construction taking an estimated three years. More recent figures from the National Audit Office show that the final cost was in the region of £152 million including the 'special requirements' of the occupier, which was still within the budget allowed.

Much of the building is underground, and the remains of 17th century glass kilns, three barge houses, an inn and evidence of a river wall were all discovered during excavations. The building has no fewer than sixty separate roof areas, and required twelve thousand square metres of glass and aluminium cladding to cover the six perimeter and internal atria. To help prevent electronic eavesdropping and jamming, as well as to stop more conventional terrorist attacks, twenty-five types of glass, along with specially designed doors, were used in construction. The building was completed in April 1994 and opened by Queen Elizabeth II in July the same year.

Establishing shots of the building are seen in *GoldenEye* and *Die Another Day*, but it has a rather more central role in *The World Is Not Enough* and *Skyfall*. In the former film Sir Robert King is killed by booby-trapped money just after leaving M's office. The explosion blows a hole in the side of the building, through which an assassin in a speedboat on the river below shoots at Bond, who launches the Q boat from within the building via a torpedo chute and gives chase (for details of the ensuing boat chase see pages 137-147). This sequence was filmed at Pinewood Studios (see Volume 2), using a fifty foot-high model. In *Skyfall* the breach of security is even more serious, as ex-agent Raoul Silver manages to hack into the building's computer network and cause an explosion, killing several employees. This sequence was filmed on Vauxhall Bridge (see previous section), but the explosion itself was computer generated during post-production.

WATERLOO - THE OLD VIC TUNNELS
WESTMINSTER BRIDGE*

[The Old Vic Tunnels where MI6 evaluate their agents]

Waterloo Bridge, connecting the north and south banks of the Thames, was opened in 1817. Its name commemorates the Battle of Waterloo, which ended the Napoleonic wars in 1815. The present bridge, designed by Giles Gilbert Scott, was completed in 1945. The area on the south bank, originally called Lambeth Marsh, is now known as Waterloo. The marsh was drained in the 18th century, but the street called Lower Marsh, now a conservation area, is a link with the past.

In 1845 the London & South Western Railway obtained powers to build a terminus at York Road, close to Waterloo Bridge, and it was only with the opening of the railway station that the area as a whole became known as Waterloo. The line was extended over Lambeth Marsh from Nine Elms by means of a curved brick viaduct of some two hundred-and-ninety brick arches.

The first design was for a through station, since it was always the intention of the railway company to terminate in the City of London. In 1864 the

---

* Also served by Westminster Underground station.

South Eastern Railway extended its railway line from London Bridge to what is now Waterloo East station. There was also a further station, Necropolis, run by the London Necropolis Company, which from 1854 ran daily funeral express trains from here to Brookwood Cemetery at a cost of two shillings and six pence per coffin. The direct link to the City of London was eventually achieved in 1898, but not quite as the railway companies wanted, since it was a single stop tube line to Bank. Waterloo station grew rather haphazardly over the years, and by the end of the Victorian period, when it was handling seven hundred trains a day, it was described as 'the most perplexing railway station in London'. Plans were soon put forward for a new, more streamlined, station, which was opened by Queen Mary in 1922. There were twenty-one platforms, only the roof and the associated supporting walls and columns for platforms eighteen to twenty-one being utilised from the original station. The main pedestrian entrance arch of Portland Stone is also a memorial to the staff killed during World War I, with statues depicting War and Peace below a wave-ruling Britannia. The arches under the station became air raid shelters during World War II while the station suffered considerable bombing. In 1990 platforms twenty and twenty-one were lost as five new platforms were constructed under a four hundred metre roof of glass and steel for the new Eurostar services, which were to operate from here between 1994 and 1997. Since these trains were transferred to the new terminus at St. Pancras this part of the station has remained unused, save for a period when it briefly became a theatre for a production of *The Railway Children*, which involved the use of a steam locomotive (propelled by a diesel) pulling one of the original carriages from the 1970 film of the same name.

The station can be seen in around thirty-five film and television productions, the most notable being *Waterloo Bridge* (1940), *Seven Days to Noon* (1950), *The Good Die Young* (1954), *The Wreck of the Mary Deare* (1959), *Terminus* (1961), *Arabesque* (1966), and *The Bourne Ultimatum* (2007).

[The almost hidden entrances to The Old Vic Tunnels in Leake Street (left) and Station Approach Road (right)]

However, it is the arches under the station that are of interest to the James Bond enthusiast. Many still remain blocked off, while others are currently being used as storage areas, car parking and the like. Leake Street, which runs under the main station, but since the demise of Eurostar trains is now just a pedestrian tunnel some three hundred metres in length, has been given over to graffiti art, and it is here that one of the entrances to The Old Vic Tunnels will be found, the other being signposted in Lower Marsh but actually on Station Approach Road (where the stage door is also located).

The complex comprises five tunnels (Nos. 228 to 232), including a purpose-built screening room, of some thirty thousand square feet in all, forming a mystical labyrinth that is fast becoming one of London's leading underground arts venues. This is all under the auspices of the Old Vic Theatre Trust, which acquired the tunnels from the former British Railways in 2010. They are available for hire for theatre, live music, cabaret, cinema, album launches, photographic shoots etc., having a capacity for eight-hundred-and-fifty people. The Old Vic Tunnels was presented the Big Society Award by Prime Minister, David Cameron, in 2011.

In *Skyfall* MI6 relocates to these tunnels after the bombing at Vauxhall Cross, and it is here that Bond undergoes his fitness evaluation. In the film, the entrance to the tunnels is some miles away, at Smithfield (page 74). We should also mention that the later scene in which a tube train crashes through the ceiling of an underground chamber was filmed on a studio set at Pinewood (see Volume 2). Two full-size carriages, each weighing about seven tonnes, were constructed and filmed remotely, since the stunt was considered too dangerous to allow the cameramen to be present. Instead ten remotely operated cameras were placed in various positions in the hope that between them they would capture the required footage without being destroyed themselves. The viewer will notice that the train is marked as 'Out of Service', and carries no passengers. The driver, who may or may not survive the crash, is computer generated.

This sequence may have been inspired by a scene intended for *On Her Majesty's Secret Service*, which would have followed Bond's meeting with Sir Hilary Bray at the College of Arms (page 79). Bond was to discover that Phidian, Sir Hilary's assistant, was actually working for Blofeld and had recorded their conversation. Bond would pursue Phidian across the roof of the College of Arms and through the streets of London, to the King Edward Street post office and sorting depot, and down to the Post Office Underground Railway, then still operational (it was not decommissioned until 2003). In a fight on the tracks Phidian is killed, but in order to make his death seem like an accident MI6 later stages an elaborate train crash at St. Pancras Station. In the final cut, the only evidence of this half-filmed sequence is the front-page headline in a copy of the *Daily Express*, carried by the MI6 man Campbell as he watches the train carrying Bond, now disguised as Sir Hilary, arrive at Lauterbrunnen in the Swiss Alps. It reads, '18 people killed in rush-hour rail crash'.

[The Coade Stone Lion at Westminster Bridge, beneath which is the entrance to Vauxhall Cross Tube station]

The Bond connection with Westminster Bridge is at the eastern end, which, rather confusingly, is on the South Bank of the river, so although Westminster Underground station is actually closer to the bridge we shall deal with it here rather than under the City of Westminster. Besides, the bridge also has a connection with the SIS Building (or more accurately the fictional disused Vauxhall Cross station which in *Die Another Day* is part of the building), already covered in this section.

The growth in importance of Westminster in the 18th century increased the need for a bridge across the river to Lambeth, since at that time the nearest bridges were London Bridge to the east or Putney Bridge to the west. The alternative was to take a boat, or the horse ferry situated where Lambeth Bridge now stands. As early as 1722 Colen Campbell submitted a bridge design, but it was rejected, along with other designs such as that by Hawksmoor in 1738. The reason was not in the design but the vested interests of the City Corporation (who would lose the tolls from London Bridge), the watermen (who would lose income from ferry crossings) and not least of all the Archbishop of Canterbury (who owned the horse ferry between Lambeth and Millbank). Collectively they held out until 1738 when Charles Labelye was appointed engineer, and building began, but not before a payment of £25,000 was made to the watermen, and a further £21,025 to the Archbishop of Canterbury. It was to be a masonry bridge with piers founded in caissons.

Building did not go smoothly, as in 1747 there was an alarming settlement of one of the piers. Labelye was blamed and called an 'unsolvent, ignorant arrogating Swiss'. The bridge was finally opened in 1750 and there was obviously pride in the structure since dogs were not allowed on the bridge and anybody found defacing the walls was subject to 'death without the benefit of clergy'. In 1802 the poet Wordsworth wrote 'Earth has not anything to show more fair: Dull would he be of soul who could pass by A sight so touching in its majesty'.

In 1823 Thomas Telford conducted a technical examination, as there were persistent problems with the settlement of the piers, and in 1836 a Parliamentary committee met to discuss the situation. The following year James Walker was commissioned to encase all the piers in cofferdams and rebuild them on piled foundations

However, no sooner had the work been completed than Parliament in its wisdom decided that a new bridge should be built. This time it was to be a cast-iron bridge of seven arches, designed by Sir Charles Barry, and built by Thomas Page between 1854 and 1862. In its time the span of twenty-five metres between parapets was exceptional.

The bridge is predominantly green in colour, the same colour as the leather seats in the House of Commons, which is on the side of the Palace of Westminster closest to the bridge, whereas Lambeth Bridge is painted red, the colour of the seats in the House of Lords, which is closest to that bridge.

At the southern end a lion of Coade Stone (an artificial almost weatherproof terracotta named after Eleanor Coade who manufactured it in her Lambeth factory) by W. F. Woodington was added much later, while at the northern end a statue of Boudicca and her daughters in a chariot by Thomas Thornycroft was unveiled in 1902. The lion, which stands on a four metre-high plinth, is itself nearly four metres tall and weighs some thirteen tonnes. Under one of its paws are inscribed the initials of the sculptor, William F. Woodington, and the date, 24 May 1837. The lion was originally painted red and stood on the parapet of the Red Lion Brewery, on the Lambeth bank of the Thames. When the brewery was demolished in 1950, to make way for the South Bank Site of the 1951 Festival of Britain, the Lion was taken down, at the request of King George VI, and moved to the entrance of Waterloo Station. It was moved again to its present site in 1966. There was actually a second lion at the brewery, which was also saved and can now be seen, painted gold, above the Rowland Hill Memorial Gate at Twickenham Stadium.

In *Die Another Day* Bond is presented with a key after his fencing duel with Gustav Graves at Blades (page 103) and proceeds to the door on the steps behind the Coade Stone lion which the key fits. This it transpires is the secret entrance to the disused Vauxhall Cross Tube station (which has never existed) where M is waiting for him. This is also where Q has a workshop, and where Bond then receives his new almost invisible Aston Martin 'Vanish' car. If you visit today you will be disappointed, for the door only leads to a broom cupboard where cleaning materials are kept.

[The Entrance to Vauxhall Cross]

Just a little further along the embankment, through the tunnel in the centre of the picture on page 54, and on the other side of Westminster Bridge is the spot where the famous black and white promotional photograph for George Lazenby in *On Her Majesty's Secret Service* was taken. Lazenby is seen leaning against a lamp post, posing with his Walther PPK gun, with 'Big Ben' framed perfectly in the background.

BOROUGH OF LEWISHAM

NEW CROSS - PARKSIDE BUSINESS ESTATE

Lewisham, in the south-east of the capital, is classed as an inner London borough. Lewisham incorporates the former Borough of Deptford, including, since 1996, the old Royal Dockyard, now known as Convoys Wharf. Notable landmarks in the borough include the Clock Tower in Lewisham High Street, Blackheath Common, the Horniman Museum and Dietrich Bonhoeffer Church at Forest Hill, Broadway Theatre at Catford, and Millwall Football Club's stadium the Den.

[Just the place to find an Aston Martin? (top). In *Skyfall* Bond and M are seen setting off for Scotland and passing under the double-arched railway bridge in Arklow Road (bottom)]

New Cross takes its name from an old hostelry and coaching house that bore the sign of a golden cross. A few good Georgian houses survive in the area, but by far the most remarkable building is the former Royal Navy School for the sons of impecunious officers, now Goldsmiths' College. It was built in a grand symmetrical Wren pastiche style, and was opened in 1843 by Prince Albert. Two residents were Robert Browning, who in the 1840s lived at Telegraph Cottage, named after the near by signalling station used by the Admiralty to send semaphore messages between London, Deal and Dover, and Sir Barnes Wallis, who grew up at No. 241 New Cross Road.

Around ten minutes walk from New Cross station will be found the Parkside Business Estate, which runs beside, and under, the main railway line between Rolt Street in the north, and Arklow Road to the south. It is the southern end by the Lord Palmerston public house that is of interest to the James Bond enthusiast, for it is here in one of the lock-up garages (No. 7 naturally) that Bond keeps his Aston Martin DB5, in which he drives M to in *Skyfall*. They turn right out of the garage and into Arklow Road, passing under the distinctive double arches of the railway bridge, through the New Cross one way system and then via Canary Wharf on their way to Skyfall.

BOROUGH OF NEWHAM

GALLIONS REACH - BECKTON GAS WORKS

Newham, formed from the former county boroughs of East Ham and West Ham, became world-famous in 2012 as the home of the Olympic Stadium and much of the Olympic Park. The population of Newham is one of the country's most ethnically diverse, with less than twenty per cent registered as white British or white Irish. Famous local residents have included Terence Stamp (actor), David Bailey (photographer), Vera Lynn (singer), Elizabeth Fry (prison reformer), Joseph Lister (pioneer of antiseptic surgery), Christine Ohuruogu and Mohammed Farah (Olympic athletes), David Essex (singer) and Honor Blackman (actress and Bond girl).

The heavily industrialised area to the north and east of the Royal Docks included the largest gas works in Europe at Beckton. The name was derived from Simon Adams Beck, who was the governor of the Gas Light and Coke Company when the site was first developed in November 1868. The plant was built to make and supply coal gas and coke. Each year from 1876 to 1970, another company nearby, Burt, Boulton and Haywood at Silvertown, distilled twelve million imperial gallons of coal tar to manufacture ingredients for a wide variety of products, including ink, dyes, mothballs, fertilisers and sulphuric acid. In 1879 the Gas Light and Coke Company set up a subsidiary, Beckton Products Works, to process the by-products rather than sell them to an independent factory. However, when the country changed from coal gas to North Sea natural gas, the main Beckton site became redundant. It was closed in 1969, and the last train to leave the by-products works departed on the 1st June 1970.

[Until recently the only structure resembling a chimney in Beckton was at Gallions Reach Shopping Park, with what remains of the former gas works, as seen in *For Your Eyes Only*, in the background]

[The site, east to west, as it appeared in the 1950s with the 'Blofeld' chimney from *For Your Eyes Only* clearly evident (top). Today all that remain are some of the gas holders (bottom). This shot, east to west, looks towards where the 'Blofeld' chimney once stood]

The site by any standards was enormous, covering some 550-acres and extending from the River Thames up to what is now Gallions Reach Shopping Park. The location was well chosen, since here beside Barking Creek the water was deep enough for steam colliers to unload coal that they had brought direct from the mines in the north-east of England (and also for ships to take away the by-products of the works for export). Two deep-water piers were built and by the 1930s an average of one millions tonnes of coal, mainly from the Durham coalfields, was unloaded at the main pier every year. At the other pier a further seven hundred and fifty thousands tonnes of coal was transferred to smaller barges destined for other works. The company ran a fleet of seventeen coastal colliers, and the site had a storage capacity for two-hundred-and-fifty-thousand tonnes of coal. In addition there was an extensive railway system, at least forty miles in length, feeding into the national network at Custom House. The line closed to passengers in 1940 following an aid raid, and to freight traffic in 1971. Of course, where there is any mineral extraction process there is also a waste product, and in this case the toxic spoil was deposited in heaps beside the main London to Tilbury road (the A13), and became known locally as the Beckton Alps. Over the years the area was landscaped and reduced in size, although from 1989 to 2001 the remaining largest heap became a dry ski slope opened by Diana, Princess of Wales. Presently derelict, it is still the highest point in Newham (and the highest artificial hill in London), a Site of Importance for Nature Conservation, and has been listed as a Site of Borough Importance for Nature Conservation, Grade II.

The opening scene of *For Your Eyes Only* was filmed at Beckton Gas Works. The pilot of Blofeld's helicopter is dead, Bond is trapped inside, and the wheelchair-bound Blofeld himself is operating the craft by remote control. Today all that remains of the complex is a few gas holders. The huge building through which Bond manages to pilot the helicopter, and the tall chimney into which he deposits Blofeld have long since disappeared. Most of the area over which the aerial sequence was filmed is now occupied by a Docklands Light Railway train depot, and the rest of the site is taken up by an industrial estate and the Gallions Reach Shopping Park. Six years earlier, the climax of the John Wayne film *Brannigan* was shot here, with of one of the railway signal boxes featuring prominently. Later movies to make good use of the site included the 1984 version of Orwell's *Nineteen Eighty-Four* and *Biggles* (1986), and it featured in pop videos for Oasis, the Smiths, the Outfield, Loop and Marcella Detroit. Its most notable screen appearance was in the Vietnam War drama *Full Metal Jacket* (1987), for which the director Stanley Kubrick had parts of the complex demolished and the rest dressed to represent the Vietnamese city of Huê. The last hour of the film, right up to the final scene in which the soldiers march off into the sunset, against the background of the burning gas works, was all done at Beckton.

BOROUGH OF SOUTHWARK

CANADA WATER - HARMSWORTH QUAYS PRINTING LIMITED

[One of the print works owned by the Carver Media Group Network]

The London Borough of Southwark lies on the southern side of the River Thames, from Blackfriars Bridge in the west to Rotherhithe in the east, and as far south as Dulwich. It is connected to the City of London by Blackfriars Bridge, the Millennium Footbridge, Southwark Bridge, London Bridge, Tower Bridge and the Rotherhithe Tunnel. Notable structures within the borough include Southwark Cathedral, Dulwich Picture Gallery (the oldest public art gallery in Britain), the Tate Modern Gallery, Shakespeare's Globe Theatre, the Imperial War Museum, Borough Market, City Hall (home of the Greater London Authority), and the Shard London Bridge (the tallest building in Europe).

The historic heart of Southwark is, confusingly, known as the Borough, situated as it is opposite the City of London. Since Roman times it was the main entry point into London, as it was here that the roads from Dover and Chichester (Watling Street and Stane Street) met. In its heyday the Borough was home to many taverns and coaching inns, most notably the Tabard (meeting place of Chaucer's pilgrims), the Queen's Head (whose sale netted John Harvard money enough to endow the university that bears his name), and London's only remaining galleried inn, the George (rebuilt in 1676 and now owned by the National Trust).

The economy of Southwark was never a threat to either the City of London or what is now termed Docklands, but it was still an important trading area, with a number of docks including Greenland Dock, Brunswick Quay and Baltic Quays (all part of Surrey Commercial Docks, now know as Surrey Quays and given over to major residential schemes in the 1980s). In addition, close to Tower Bridge and the City of London there were major warehousing developments at Butler's Wharf and Hay's Wharf.

Today the press and publishing industry is well represented in the borough; the Financial Times has its head office in Southwark Bridge Road, with Express Group Newspapers close by in Blackfriars Road and IPC Magazines in Southwark Street. Further out at Canada Water is where the *Evening Standard* and *Daily Mail* are currently printed at the fourteen-acre site of Harmsworth Quays Printing Limited, although by the end of 2013 they will have relocated to a new £50 million site at Thurrock in Essex, the interests of the Daily Mail General Trust having been sold to British Land in 2012 (who aim to further redevelop the Surrey Quays area along with Southwark Council, which owns the freehold to much of the land).

In 1988 Harmsworth Quays Printing Limited moved to flexographic printing, installing eight shaftless KBA Courier presses at its Canada Water site. These enable production of one hundred and twenty-eight page editions of *The Daily Mail*, with sixty-four pages in full colour. The presses can turn out eighty thousand copies an hour – about two million each day. The great advantage of the system is the use of water-based inks, providing high net production, with brilliant colour, strong rub resistance and reduced wastage. The plant is now the biggest flexo print operator in the world.

[The state-of-the-art printing presses at Harmsworth Quays]

Harmsworth Quays, then, was the natural choice for Elliot Carver's printing house in *Tomorrow Never Dies*. Most of it, anyway. The chase and fight scenes at the works are a montage of footage shot here, at West Ferry Printers (page 64) and at Feltham (covered in Volume 2). Basically, all the shots without windows and those in which the printing presses are visible were filmed at Harmsworth Quays.

BOROUGH OF TOWER HAMLETS

CROSSHARBOUR - WEST FERRY PRINTERS

Tower Hamlets encompasses much of what is known as the East End, from the City of London to Canary Wharf on the Isle of Dogs, including areas of Bethnal Green, Stepney and Poplar. The borough owes its name to an Order in Council for a muster of the men of those hamlets 'which owe their service to the Tower'. In 1605 the right of the Lieutenant of the Tower of London to exact guard duty was confirmed, and the area was designated a military unit with the name Tower Hamlets. Twenty-one hamlets were recorded in 1720, most of their names now surviving in stations on the Underground. A Borough of Tower Hamlets existed between 1832 and 1918, and the name was revived in 1965 for the present London Borough.

The opening of the docks and associated industries attracted numerous unskilled and semi-skilled labourers to the area, while providing low wages and poor living conditions. The railways improved matters somewhat, by offering the opportunity to work in the East End but live further out, in the newer suburbs of Essex. Thus began a steady decline in population throughout the 20th century, though numbers have risen since 2001 from less than two hundred thousand to more than two hundred and fifty thousand. The whole of the East End suffered much bomb damage during World War II, the docks, railways and industry being obvious targets. The 1950s saw new housing projects, under the Abercrombie Plan for London, while the 1970s saw the decline of the docks, with the closure of the last East End dock in 1980. This was also the date of the founding of the London Docklands Development Corporation, which has been responsible for regeneration of certain areas such as Canary Wharf and parts of the Olympic Park, though other districts continue to experience some of the worst poverty in the country. The area has always been known for immigrants, be they Huguenots in the 17th century, East European Jews in the 19th century, or Bangladeshis in the 20th century.

Crossharbour, just to the south of Canary Wharf, lies next to Millwall outer dock, which made an appearance in the boat chase pre-title sequence of *The World Is Not Enough* (pages 137-147). Along the northern side of the dock is West Ferry Printers, a subsidiary of the Express Newspapers Group. At the time it was completed in 1986 it was Europe's largest and most efficient newspaper printing plant, occupying a fourteen-acre site, and with the capacity to print around twenty million newspapers a week. The site was a pioneer in print automation, using state-of-the-art robot operations, which became an industry benchmark for efficiency and quality. At its peak the plant used three thousand tonnes of paper, sixty tonnes of ink and thirty thousand printing plates per week. However, after twenty-four years of operation it was announced in 2010 that the site was to close with printing being moved to Luton, where £100 million would be spent on the latest hybrid coldset and heatset presses over a five-year period.

The other sides of the dock are given over to several housing developments and impressive apartment towers. Clippers Quay housing estate is located around the old dry dock, while the Mill Quay development is on the site of an old flour mill. At the west end of the dock is the Docklands Sailing and Watersports Centre, which runs a fleet of training dinghies.

[West Ferry Printers at Millwall outer dock showing the roof where Bond gained entry to Carver's Hamburg printing works]

In *Tomorrow Never Dies* Bond breaks into the Hamburg print works of the Carver Media Group Network. He gains entry, with the help of his modified mobile telephone, from the roof of the building. These scenes were not done in Germany but were actually filmed at West Ferry Printers. There is a clue in that some of the sailing centre dinghies are in the background. However, once inside filming switches to the IBM Building in Feltham (covered in Volume 2) and Harmsworth Quays Printing Limited at Canada Water (page 62), although shots in the printing works where there are windows in view are West Ferry.

WESTFERRY - CANARY RIVERSIDE HEALTH CLUB

[Not Shanghai, but London where Bond takes a dip in *Skyfall*]

Westferry is a small area in Limehouse centred around Westferry Road, which runs down the west side of the Isle of Dogs, past the western end of Millwall outer dock, and ending as it becomes Manchester Road by Island Gardens in the south. The name alludes to a one-time passenger ferry (and later a horse ferry as well), run by the Greenwich watermen, which existed at the southern tip of the Isle of Dogs. Since the closure of the West India and Millwall Docks and the construction of Canary Wharf, the road has changed beyond recognition. Where once there was industry are now apartment blocks, warehouse and wharf conversions, along with other leisure developments along the riverside. The Italianate St. Paul's Presbyterian Church, built for Scottish ship workers in 1859, has been saved from dereliction and sensitively converted into an arts and performance centre called The Space. Further along, and also preserved, is Burrell's Wharf where Brunel's *Great Eastern* steamship was launched with difficulty.

Also noteworthy are the Canary Riverside residential, hotel and retail developments, which lie either side of the intensively landscaped Westferry Circus, created between 1987 and 1991 as the main access roundabout for Canary Wharf. Behind the Four Seasons hotel is the Canary Riverside Club, a Virgin Active Centre, featuring an infinity swimming pool with large windows looking out across the River Thames. In *Skyfall* this is the pool, apparently atop of a hotel in Shanghai, where Bond takes a swim with the view being added digitally.

CITY OF LONDON
BANK - DRAPERS' HALL

The City of London covers some 677-acres, or slightly over a square mile, and is ruled over by the Lord Mayor and Corporation of London. Today it has a population of less than seven thousand residents, most of whom live in the Barbican complex, and is seen as a place with many centuries of history, traditions of craft guilds and commerce, state pageantry and national hospitality, and an exemplary system of local government that stands as an example of careful husbandry, civic pride and national dignity.

It was a settlement long before the arrival of the Romans, who recognised its importance, for in 67AD Tacitus wrote that Londinium was a 'flourishing trading city'. Archaeological evidence has shown that there was a Great Basilica and Forum (in Leadenhall), an amphitheatre (where the Guildhall now stands) and a temple to Mithras (in Bucklersbury). The Romans also built a defensive wall (fragments of which still survive) of over 3 miles in length, with six main gates, to mark the boundaries of the City.

The legions withdrew in AD 410. There was a Saxon settlement here in the 6th century, and in 604 King Ethelbert of Kent founded St. Paul's Cathedral. His palace in the City was occupied by successive kings until in 1060 Edward the Confessor moved his court to Westminster. Upon his arrival in 1066, William the Conqueror built the Tower of London just outside the eastern wall, to keep the citizens under surveillance, though he confirmed the rights they had enjoyed under King Edward. In 1215, besides the Magna Carta, King John signed a document entitling the City to government by an elected Mayor and corporation. This was the period in which the craft guilds and livery companies became prominent.

After years of political and religious turmoil, the reign of Elizabeth I saw London become a world trading centre, thanks largely to Sir Thomas Gresham, who restored the English currency and built the Royal Exchange as a forum for City merchants. Great international export companies were founded, including, in 1600, the Honourable East India Company, which maintained an army and a navy in India and developed a mercantile fleet with unprecedented standards of service, discipline and maintenance. The arts and architecture also flourished in the City, as the names of Chaucer, Shakespeare, Inigo Jones, Wren and Hogarth bear witness.

Buildings were mostly small, cramped and ill-constructed with primitive sanitation, so no wonder it was said that with a westerly wind London could be smelt from Tilbury. The consequence of this was disease (which spread rapidly), and in 1666 the Great Fire of London, which was to destroy two-thirds of the City, including the Royal Exchange and St. Paul's Cathedral. This was a blessing in disguise for it allowed the architects appointed by a commission to design better buildings made of brick and stone. In the following century more handsome buildings sprang up, such as the Bank of England and the Mansion House. The Victorians continued in the same way with infrastructure also being of importance. This era saw the construction of Tower Bridge, the replacement of London and Blackfriars Bridges and the introduction of the railways and Underground. By the end of the 19th century the City could boast no fewer than four mainline termini, at Liverpool Street, Fenchurch Street, Cannon Street and Holborn Viaduct.

Throughout the 19th century, the City served as the world's primary business centre, and remains a major meeting point for businesses to this day, with around three hundred thousand people working within the City bounds. The legal profession forms a major component of the northern and western sides of the City, especially in the Temple and Chancery Lane areas where the Inns of Court are located. Meanwhile the insurance industry is focussed around the eastern boundary, with Lloyd's of London established in the vicinity of Leadenhall Street. At the very heart of all this is the area of Bank, named after the Bank of England, though it isn't the only bank here, since there are in fact over five hundred banking groups represented within the City. Bank Underground station is the eighth busiest in London, and being serviced by five lines, as well as the Docklands Light Railway, makes it possible to get quickly to most parts of London.

From the north-east corner of the Bank of England, head east along Throgmorton Street and you will quickly reach Drapers' Hall, home of the Worshipful Company of Drapers, which ranks third among the City's Livery Companies. Its charter was granted in 1364, though an association of Drapers is known to have existed in the 12th century, as the wool trade was of very high importance in the middle ages, and the company's members dealt in both import and export of woollen cloth. The first hall, recorded as early as 1425, stood in St. Swithin's Lane. The second, on the present site, was purchased from King Henry VIII, to whom it had been forfeit upon the execution of Thomas Cromwell in 1543. In 1660, when General Monk was preparing the way for the Restoration of Charles II, he had his headquarters here. The hall was destroyed in the Great Fire of 1666, and rebuilt the next year by Edward Jerman. After further damage by fire in 1772, the front was remodelled by the Adam brothers. There was further work done between 1868 and 1870, and again in 1898. The only parts surviving from 1772 are the magnificent Court Dining Room, with its fine plaster ceiling, and the Clerks' Office.

[The Livery Hall, where Ourumov makes his report in *GoldenEye*]

For the James Bond enthusiast, however, the Livery Hall is the focus of interest. It was enlarged to its present size by Herbert Williams in the 1860s, surrounded by twenty-eight columns of polished granite, between which are displayed the Company's collection of royal portraits. At the northern end, the room is adorned by Richard Belt's statue *Hypatia* and a copy of John Gibson's *The Tinted Venus*, and the ceiling panels feature scenes from *The Tempest* and *A Midsummer Night's Dream*, as well as representations of History, Science, Ethics and Literature. These are the work of the neo-classical painter Herbert Draper, and date from the first decade of the 20th century. In *GoldenEye*, it is to this room, supposedly in St. Petersburg, that General Ourumov is summoned after the destruction of the Severnaya space research station – from which Ourumov himself has stolen the GoldenEye access key. Here he learns that Natalya Simonova has also survived the attack, but he assures the meeting that there is not a second GoldenEye electromagnetic pulse satellite weapon (though in fact there is).

BARBICAN - FROBISHER CRESCENT
LONDON WALL
SMITHFIELD MARKET

[Frobisher Crescent with Cromwell Tower behind. It is here that M finds out that Slate was a 'dead end' in *Quantum of Solace*]

World War II outdid the damage of the Great Fire of London, with the Guildhall and everything around it to the north between Aldersgate and Moorgate (some 35-acres) being completely burnt out and laid waste. This was the area now known as Barbican. It was noted that 'one could walk for over half a mile without passing a single standing structure'. Initially the Corporation of London wanted to redevelop the area for commercial use only, but by 1956 it was made clear by government that it should be a 'genuine residential neighbourhood, incorporating schools, shops, open spaces and amenities'. The architects Peter Chamberlin, Geoffry Powell and Christopher Bon, who had set up practice in 1952 had the final version of their plan accepted in 1959, with structural engineers Arup commencing site clearance in 1960. This not only included the removal of remaining buildings but also of all existing roads, sewers, gas and electricity mains along with the rerouting and encasing in tunnels of four railway tracks belonging to the Circle and Metropolitan railway.

Building of the 2,104 flats of the Barbican Estate finally began in 1963, although the Arts Centre was not started for another decade. The housing comprised tall towers (Lauderdale, Shakespeare and Cromwell) and long terrace blocks, constructed of aggregate concrete, arranged round large courts or piazzas and all connected by elevated walkways. Unlike other high-rise developments of the time, the Barbican was built to a high standard, with a hint of a fortress in the design. At the time the towers (two being forty-four floors high) were the tallest residential blocks in Europe. Being a mixture of one- to five-rooms, they were intended to suit everybody from the impoverished to the wealthy City worker, but since the Corporation of London started selling them off in 2000 most are now beyond the means of all but those in the upper tax bracket.

The complex also included the Barbican Arts Centre, the City of London School for Girls, and the Guildhall School of Music and Drama. The Arts Centre cost around £153 million and is generally considered to be of a less successful design than the rest of the Barbican, being criticised for its confusing maze of walkways, landings and staircases 'having no immediately apparent correspondence with the venues they serve'. It comprises an art gallery over two floors, three cinemas (the largest having a capacity of two-hundred-and-eighty seats), a concert hall of three curved tiers (with a capacity of just over two thousand seats), and a thousand-seat theatre (home to the Royal Shakespeare Company until 2002). In 2012 the Centre was host to the very successful Designing 007 Fifty Years of Bond Style exhibition. Frobisher Court, on the west side of the Centre, was designed as a semi-circular block of flats, but for most of their life they have been occupied by the City of London Business School. However, in

2011 the top three floors were converted into attractive flats looking down on the Sculpture Court.

In *Quantum of Solace*, there are aerial shots of a rather crowded Sculpture Court as M emerges from Frobisher Crescent. She is in communication with Bond, now in Haiti, who has tracked down Edmund Slate (the contact for Mitchell, the double agent who was also M's former bodyguard) and killed him, much to M's displeasure.

[London Wall looking west towards One London Wall]

London Wall is a street running along the southern perimeter of Barbican between Aldersgate Street and Broad Street, along the line of the original Roman wall. At St. Alfege Garden part of the wall still remains, while beneath the west end of the street is evidence of the west gate of the Roman fort at Cripplegate. From 1329 to 1536 Elsing Spital, an Augustinian priory and hospital for one hundred blind men, stood here. At the Dissolution of the Monasteries King Henry VIII gave the priory to the parishioners of St. Alfege, whose own church was in danger of falling down.

As part of the area devastated by bombing in World War II, the original street was realigned (and renamed simply as Route XI for the city planners) before being rebuilt in the 1960s with integrated office towers and walkways. The final part of this rebuilding was the construction of the Museum of London, which opened in 1976 and was revamped in 2010. It documents the history of London from prehistoric times to the present day, and is well worth several hours of anyone's time. Admission is free. For further details see www.museumoflondon.org.uk.

Many of those 1960s office blocks have not stood the test of time and have already been replaced by structures such as Terry Farrell's pink and grey striped Alban Gate, which bridges London Wall (1992), Winchester House (1999), and the curvaceous One London Wall (2003). However, the finest building by far in the area is beneath One London Wall. This is the address of the Worshipful Company of Plaisterers, which was incorporated by charter in 1501. Their first hall was destroyed in the Great Fire of London, and the second designed by Wren also succumbed to fire in 1882. The present hall was opened in 1972 and is the largest (with a seating capacity of three hundred), and most beautifully decorated (with plasterwork in the style of Adam) of any of the livery companies' halls.

London Wall is a favourite with film companies since at weekends it is a quiet area of the City and can be easily closed off without too much disruption. Indeed, each year this is where the various floats muster prior to the Lord Mayor's Show. Productions shot here include *Sebastian* (1968), *The Rise and Rise of Michael Rimmer* (1970), *Alien Autopsy* (2006) and *Ocean's 13* (2007). In *Tomorrow Never Dies* it is along here that Bond is briefed by M in the back seat of her Daimler, complete with a four-motorcycle police escort. The car actually goes around in circles, and as the keen observer will note, it passes the same spot more than once. The car is first seen at Bank turning from Prince's Street into Poultry and along Cheapside. (This junction has also appeared in *28 Days Later* (2002) and *National Treasure: Book of Secrets* (2007) during the car chase sequence). It would then have to turn right into King Edward Street, where part of *On*

Her Majesty's Secret Service was to have been filmed (page 53), and onto London Wall, at the end of which it would turn right into Moorgate and Prince's Street to complete the circle. However, the driver must surely be lost for whereas at the start of the clip he has been travelling east along London Wall, in subsequent shots he is travelling west.

[In *Skyfall* this is the entrance to the emergency offices for MI6, but in real life was once the underground railway sidings for Smithfield Market in the background]

To the west of Barbican is Smithfield, originally Smoothfield, described in the middle ages as 'a plain grassy space just outside the City Walls'. Here, as Thomas Becket's clerk William FitzStephen wrote in 1173, 'every Friday there is a celebrated rendezvous of fine horses to be sold,' and it seems that sheep, pigs and cattle were also traded. In 1400 the City of London was granted the tolls from the market by charter.

From 1123 until its suppression in 1855 for rowdiness and debauchery, Smithfield was the site of the famous Bartholomew Fair. As a convenient open area close to the City, it was also used for tournaments, jousting and sporting events. A tournament held in 1357 was attended by the Kings of both England and France.

Here, too, Wat Tyler came with his rebels in 1381 to meet King Richard II. For Tyler the outcome was fatal: he was stabbed by the Mayor of London and then publicly beheaded. Smithfield was in fact a place of public execution for over four hundred years, criminals being hanged (or worse) 'betwixt the horse pool and the river of Wels'. In 1305 the Scottish rebel Sir William Wallace was hanged, drawn and quartered here, and during the four-year reign of Mary Tudor (1554-1558) no fewer than two hundred Protestants were burned at the stake as heretics. In the 17th century the area was notorious for fighting and duelling.

The City of London Corporation did bring some sort of order to the place by first paving it and providing sewers and railings in 1615, and then formally establishing a cattle market under Royal Charter in 1638. There were still complaints, though, about the drunken herdsmen, some of whom were inclined to high spirits and stampeding their cattle through the surrounding streets on their way to market. Often the tormented beasts took refuge in shops and houses, which is said to be the origin of the phrase 'a bull in a china shop'.

Smithfield was not a nice place to visit. In *Oliver Twist*, Charles Dickens describes the problems well enough: 'The ground was covered, nearly ankle-deep, with filth and mire; a thick steam perpetually rising from the reeking bodies of cattle ... the unwashed, unshaven, squalid and dirty figures constantly running to and fro, and bursting in and out of the throng, rendered it a stunning and bewildering scene, which quite confounded the senses'.

Finally in 1855 the sale of live cattle was moved to the Metropolitan Cattle Market in Islington. Between 1851 and 1866 Horace Jones (who was also responsible for the design of other London markets as well as Tower Bridge) developed the 10-acre site into a new market that had an underground railway linking Smithfield with the main line. Smithfield became a vast cathedral-like structure of ornamental cast iron, stone, Welsh slate and glass. It was a place full of light and air, consisting of two main buildings linked under a great roof and separated by a central arcade, the Grand Avenue.

It was opened in 1868 as the London Central Meat Market, and further extensions were made in 1875 and 1899. Part of the market was subject to fire in 1958 but was rebuilt in 1963 at a cost of £2 million. Today the market employs around one thousand, five hundred people, and sells over a hundred and fifty thousand tonnes of meat every year. Smithfield Market, like Billingsgate and New Spitalfields, has its own Market Constabulary, answerable directly to the City of London Corporation. For many decades it has had its own licensing laws too, allowing some of the local public houses to open as early as 6.30 am. In 1992 the City Corporation carried out a major refurbishment of the two main market buildings at a cost of around £80m. In this modernisation the underground area, no longer railway sidings, became a car park.

In *Skyfall* Bond is driven through the barrier guarding the entrance to the underground car park. In the film, he is on his way to the new subterranean offices into which MI6 has moved after the explosion at Vauxhall Cross. These offices must be vast, extending well over a mile south, under the Thames to Waterloo, since the interior scenes of Bond's evaluation were shot at the Old Vic Tunnels (page 51).

Other productions filmed in this part of London include *Last Orders* (2001), with Michael Caine playing a butcher, and *Dorian Gray* (2009), in which the market exterior stands in for King's Cross station. The Priory Church of St. Bartholomew the Great featured in *Sherlock Holmes* (2009) as the scene of Lord Blackwood's interrupted human sacrifice; it was also seen in *Robin Hood: Prince of Thieves* (1991), *Four Weddings and a Funeral* (1994) and *Elizabeth: The Golden Age* (2007).

LIVERPOOL STREET - BROADGATE TOWER

Liverpool Street came into existence in 1829 when the former winding street known as Old Bethlem, in which the Bethlem Hospital stood, was redeveloped. The new street was named after Lord Liverpool, who was Prime Minister from 1812 to 1827.

In 1862 the Great Eastern Railway wished to extend its line beyond the original terminus in Shoreditch and into the City. They chose a site on the north side of Liverpool Street, next to Broad Street station. The company wanted a huge building, extending as far as London Wall, but the authorities objected. Instead Edward Wilson designed a gothic red-brick terminus with platforms below street level. It opened in 1874 and was extended in 1891, increasing the number of platforms to eighteen, the most of any London station until 1908, when Victoria station was also enlarged. On the east side is the Great Eastern Hotel (now the Andaz Liverpool Street), designed by Charles Barry Jr. and Edward Middleton Barry, and opened in 1884. It was completely refurbished in the 1990s. Views of Liverpool Street station have differed. In 1944 Tom Driberg called it 'almost completely squalid', but in 1972 John Betjeman described it as 'the most picturesque and interesting of the London termini'.

[The Broadgate Tower over the tracks of Liverpool Street station]

In 1986 there was a major redevelopment, when the huge Broadgate office complex was constructed on the site of Broad Street station and beside and above the railway approaches into Liverpool Street station. All the platforms at Liverpool Street now have a common barrier line, making it brighter in appearance and much easier to navigate, but its Victorian façade, cast-iron pillars, and certain other features remain, including the Great Eastern War Memorial, relocated at street level from the old main booking office. The original unveiling in 1922 was performed by Field Marshal Sir Henry Wilson, MP, who was assassinated by two IRA gunmen on his return home from the ceremony.

Also on the upper level is a small plaque commemorating the filming here of *Mission Impossible* in 1996. Liverpool Street station also features in *The File of the Golden Goose* (1969), *The Elephant Man* (1980), *The Dogs of War* (1980), *Mona Lisa* (1986), *Bridget Jones's Diary* (2001), *Alex Rider: Stormbreaker* (2006), *Brick Lane* (2007), *St. Trinian's 2: The Legend of Fritton's Gold* (2009) and *Egression* (2011).

[The Primrose Street entrance to The Broadgate Tower]

The thirty-five floors of the Broadgate Tower, built between 2005 and 2009 by Skidmore, Owings and Merrill, over major railway lines heading into Liverpool Street station, make it one of London's tallest skyscrapers at one hundred and sixty-five metres. As it sits on a large construction raft that has been built above the entrance to the station (taking advantage of 'air rights') the groundwork took longer than would usually be the case, as work could not be allowed to interfere with the running of the train services. However, its steel core permitted a quicker finish than a concrete core would have done. It was archaeology that held up construction for several years, as many ancient artefacts were found on the site. The cost of construction is estimated at £240 million.

The tower's distinctive external diagonal steel beams enhance its appearance of strength, similar to that of the Bank of China Tower in Hong Kong. No doubt this is why it was chosen by the producers of *Skyfall* to represent the skyscraper in Shanghai to which Bond pursues the assassin Patrice.

Bond, in his car, watches Patrice approach the skyscraper from Primrose Street, across a large plaza, landscaped with trees. The reception area, where Patrice kills the security guard, is finished in polished granite, coloured glass and stainless steel, with escalators rising to two lobbies, lined with travertine limestone, from which double-decker lifts provide access to all floors. Bond is seen ascending on one of the Broadgate Tower escalators, but the stunt involving the lifts was filmed back at Pinewood Studios (covered in Volume 2).

MANSION HOUSE - COLLEGE OF ARMS

Despite the name, Mansion House Underground station is not at the Mansion House, but at the junction of Queen Victoria Street and Cannon Street. The station closest to the Mansion House (directly opposite, in fact) is Bank. The reason is that when the station was opened in 1871 as the eastern terminus of the Metropolitan District Railway, the Mansion House was the nearest major building, and as it is the official residence of the Lord Mayor of London, located at the very heart of the City, the choice of name was obvious. Bank Underground station did not come into being until 1900 (the one-stop Waterloo and City line opened in 1898, but its terminus by the Bank of England was named simply City). From 1883 there was a service from Mansion House to Windsor, via Ealing, but it proved unprofitable and was closed two years later.

Between 1867 and 1871, the Metropolitan District Railway was extended from Blackfriars station on the Victoria Embankment (opened in 1870) to Mansion House station, using the cut-and-cover method. What covered the line was the newly constructed Queen Victoria Street, which continued on to the Bank of England.

[Entrance to the College of Arms in Queen Victoria Street]

At the western end of the street is the church of St. Andrew-by-the-Wardrobe, rebuilt to Sir Christopher Wren's original designs after severe damage during World War II. Further along, opposite the College of Arms, is another Wren church, the pretty little St. Benet Paul's Wharf. In 1902 London's first GPO telephone exchange opened in Faraday Buildings on the site of Doctors' Commons (former home of England's Admiralty, Probate, and principal Ecclesiastical Court), though the present building mostly dates from the early 1930s. Between Mansion House station and the Bank are the foundations of the Roman Temple of Mithras, behind which, on the corner of Walbrook and Cannon Street is the futuristic Walbrook Building, which featured as the headquarters of MI6 in the 2011 spy spoof *Johnny English Reborn*.

The various Victorian offices in the street have now largely been replaced by modern blocks, although Darcy House (built in 1867) still stands and is today the United Kingdom headquarters of the Church of Scientology, while close by at No. 101, beside the pedestrian approach to the Millennium Bridge, is the new International Headquarters of the Salvation Army. There are no skyscrapers here since the height and profile of the street's buildings are constrained by the requirement to preserve sightlines to St. Paul's Cathedral.

The most impressive building in the street is that of the College of Arms, which dates from the 17th century. The College is the official repository of the coats of arms and pedigrees of English, Welsh, Northern Irish and Commonwealth families and their descendants. The officers of the College, known as heralds, specialise in genealogical and heraldic work for their clients (who can be individuals or corporations), with coats of arms still being granted by Letters Patent from the senior heralds, the Kings of Arms. The hereditary head of the College of Arms is the Earl Marshal, whose responsibilities include the arrangement of coronations, State funerals and the State Opening of Parliament.

In 1555 the heralds were allocated a house called Derby Place, which stood on the present site. Like many City buildings, it was destroyed in the Great Fire in 1666, but fortunately the College records were saved, and taken to temporary premises at the Palace of Westminster.

A shortage of funds meant that reconstruction could not begin until 1670, the costs being financed in stages and the building work proceeding slowly in parts. A good amount came from the heralds' own purses, but a significant sum was raised by subscriptions from noble donors, records of whose names survive in a series of lavish volumes known as the Benefactors Books.

[The Court of Chivalry through, which Bond passes on his way to meet Sir Hilary Bray in *On Her Majesty's Secret Service*]

The new building was to have a uniform height of three storeys, divided by plain brick string courses, with a basement and attic storey in addition. There was a hall, a porter's lodge, and a waiting room, with the rest of the space in the building being given over to the accommodation of the heralds, most of whom had several rooms. The hall, now known as the Earl Marshal's Court, was used as a library until at least 1699, and soon afterwards was furnished as the Court of Chivalry, as it remains today.

In around 1742 a sugar refinery was built immediately abutting the College to the northeast. This, regarded as a high fire risk, was a source of constant anxiety to the heralds until 1818 when they were finally able to buy the property, which in turn was redeveloped as a new record room.

The original plans for Queen Victoria Street would have resulted in the complete demolition of the College. The heralds naturally protested, and in the event only parts of the south-west and south-east wings were pulled down, leaving the College as a three-sided building whose open courtyard faced the new Queen Victoria Street. The old entrance on Benet's Hill was closed off and the present entrance porch, with its terrace and steps, was constructed. The splendid wrought iron gates and railings, removed from the recently demolished Goodrich Court in Herefordshire, were erected in 1956, a gift from an American benefactor.

The College of Arms has a pivotal role in *On Her Majesty's Secret Service*, when Bond learns that Blofeld is in communication with one of the genealogists, Sir Hilary Bray, as he is attempting to establish a claim to the title of Comte de Bleuchamp (de Bleuville in the original novel). As M later remarks, Blofeld 'sets great store' by his claim to an aristocratic title, adding that snobbery is 'a very curious thing'. The exterior was filmed on location, of course, but the interior scenes were done at Pinewood Studios (covered in Volume 2), partly because the script originally called for an extended sequence involving a chase over the rooftop of the College (page 79).

Ian Fleming had expert help with the heraldry in his novel from Count Robin de la Lanne-Mirrlees, Baron of Inchdrewer, Count of the Republic of San Marino, and Laird of Great Bernera. Although he later became Richmond Herald, at that time he was Rouge Dragon Pursuivant, and Fleming gave the fictional genealogist the title of Sable Basilisk Pursuivant. In the film Sable Basilisk is Sir Hilary Bray, but in the novel they are two different people.

Fleming may also have had help from Rodney Dennys, Somerset Herald, who had like Fleming served in MI6 during World War II. Indeed a recent added attraction for visitors to the College is an exhibition of some of the script pages, with hand written corrections by Dennys, for *On Her Majesty's Secret Service* which are displayed under the glass on the window sills of the Earl Marshal's Court.

TOWER HILL - PORT OF LONDON AUTHORITY BUILDING

Tower Hill was the principal place of execution by beheading for traitors who had been imprisoned in the Tower of London, often watched by thousands of spectators. Seventy-five traitors are known to have been executed in this way, from Sir Simon de Burley in 1388 to Lord Lovat in 1747. For some time afterwards gallows stood on Tower Hill, the final hangings in 1780 being those of two prostitutes and a one-armed soldier who had been arrested during the Gordon Riots. The execution site is marked by a stone in the pavement at the west end of the gardens of Trinity

Square. Also in the gardens is the Tower Hill Memorial commemorating men and women of the Merchant Navy and fishing fleets who died in both World Wars and who have no known grave. The World War I section, designed by Sir Edwin Lutyens with a sculpture by William Reid-Dick, has twelve thousand names inscribed, whereas the World War II extension, designed by Sir Edward Maufe with a sculpture by Charles Wheeler, bears almost twice as many names.

[The magnificent setting for the Prime Minister's enquiry in *Skyfall*]

The nautical theme continues along the north side of Trinity Square with two grand buildings. The smaller is Trinity House, designed by Samuel Wyatt and built between 1792 and 1794. It was severely damaged in World War II but was fully restored afterwards. The Corporation of Trinity House, granted a Royal Charter by King Henry VIII in 1514, is the body responsible for the safety of shipping and the well being of seafarers. To this end they provide in excess of six hundred aids to navigation, ranging from lighthouses to a satellite navigation service for shipping around British waters, the Channel Islands and Gibraltar. Trinity House is also the licensing authority for Deep Sea Pilots in Northern European waters.

Adjacent is the former Port of London Authority Building (No. 10 Trinity Square), erected in 1922 to the flamboyant designs of Sir Edwin Cooper. The building was described by Nicholas Pevsner as 'a lasting monument to Edwardian optimism like a super-palace for an international exhibition, showy, happily vulgar and extremely impressive'. Originally the Authority was set up in 1908 to take full control over the tidal river and its docking. This included a reduction and regularisation of docking charges (which had been responsible for London losing trade to other ports) and the dredging of the River Thames to allow large ships to enter the docks. It was also responsible for the maintenance and extension of the various London docks, and latterly the relocation downriver to the Tilbury Docks, with the introduction of containerisation. In many ways the Authority was a victim of its own success, since with the closure of the upriver docks, its task was now reduced to managing safety on the tidal Thames, and responsibility for maintaining the river channels for navigation and moorings, lights and buoys, as well as providing pilotage services. Consequently the Authority vacated Trinity Square in 1971, moving to smaller offices. Interestingly the building acted as host in 1946 to the inaugural meeting of the United Nations General Assembly.

At the end of 2010 the building was acquired from Willis Insurance by a Singapore-based development company and a Chinese investment company. Under their joint venture, Bullet Investments, the groups are converting the site into a one-hundred-and-twenty bedroom luxury hotel with a private members' club, spa and restaurants, as well as thirty-seven private luxury apartments on the top four floors. The hotel, to be known as Ten Trinity Hotel, is due to open for business in 2014.

The building may look familiar, as it has been seen on both the big and small screens, in productions such as *Two-Way Stretch* (1960), *Sweeney!* (1977), in which it was the location of the Arab oil conference, and episodes of *The Professionals*, as the implied offices of CI5, from which, at the end of the opening titles, Cowley emerges and is joined by Bodie and Doyle as they walk around Trinity Square.

At the beginning of *Skyfall*, M is summoned to this building, now doubling as a Whitehall Department, her Jaguar coming from Savage Gardens and pulling up in front of the portico with its four huge pillars. Here she is informed by Gareth Mallory of her impending retirement. She returns to the building later on, to give evidence to the Prime Minister's panel of inquiry.

Naturally the interior shots of the ensuing gunfight with Silva, who has managed to escape from MI6 custody, were filmed back at Pinewood Studios (covered in Volume 2). It is evident that the building represents a block in or near Whitehall, since, as we know, Bond is shown leaving Westminster Underground station and running up Whitehall (page 124) to protect M from Silva. If it were not so, he would have to run about three miles to Trinity Square! As it is, he makes it in time, and is seen running into the square from Cooper's Row.

Later Silva is seen exiting the side entrance and being whisked off at speed in a police car, south towards Muscovy Street (ignoring the fact that he is going the wrong way in a one-way street), while M is ushered from the building by Bond, using the same exit, to her waiting Jaguar, which speeds off in the other direction, turning right into Pepys Street, and then right again into Savage Gardens.

CITY OF WESTMINSTER

BAYSWATER* - ST. SOPHIA'S GREEK ORTHODOX CATHEDRAL

Westminster, which was made a city by royal charter in 1900, has perhaps the largest concentration of historic and important buildings in the United Kingdom, including the Palace of Westminster, Buckingham Palace and Westminster Abbey, as well as the government buildings in Whitehall and Downing Street. It includes the shopping areas of Oxford Street and Regent Street as well as what is termed Theatreland. Although the current boundaries only date from 1965, the origins of the City pre-date the

---

* Also served by Queensway Underground station.

Norman Conquest. In the mid-11th century Edward the Confessor began construction of an abbey at Westminster along with a palace between the abbey and the river, thereby guaranteeing the importance of the area. For centuries the City of Westminster, and the City of London were geographically quite distinct. Only in the 16th century did the growing urban sprawl envelop villages and hamlets, such as Marylebone and Kensington, blurring the boundaries.

Bayswater, to the south of Paddington, takes its name from Bayard's Watering, the chief of the district's springs, which served as a natural drinking place for horses. In 1439 Westminster Abbey granted a water supply from this source to the City of London via the Bayswater Conduit which was operational until 1812. The area was mainly occupied by wealthy merchants and fashionable Victorian gentry, who moved into the large houses that were being built here. Bayswater was not as affluent as Belgravia, but from the 1830s there were many fine stucco-faced mansions of four or five storeys, which over time gave way to the magnificent terraces and squares that began to dominate the area in the 1860s.

Today Bayswater is one of London's most cosmopolitan areas, augmented by a high number of hotels. Among these is a large Greek community, attracted by London's Greek Orthodox Cathedral, St. Sophia.

The church, in Moscow Road, was commissioned by a committee presided over by Emmanuel Mavrocordato, who raised £50,000 being raised for its construction over a three year period, mainly from the local Greek community which included prosperous and influential London merchants and financiers. It was designed in the Byzantine style to the design of John Oldrid Scott, whose extensive ecclesiastical architecture includes the Greek Orthodox chapel at West Norwood Cemetery. From the outside the domed roof and arched windows are quite modest, but inside it is a different matter, with elaborate decoration in polychromatic marble. Normally the walls of such a church would have frescos, but Ludwig Thiersch, who was responsible for the iconostasis, thought that the London climate would be too damp for such paintings to last for long, and so suggested that the walls should be covered in mosaics. The trustees agreed and commissioned Byzantine-inspired mosaics from G. M. Mercenero & Company, to a design by A. G. Walker, with further mosaics being commissioned in 1926 from Boris Anrep.

The church took just eighteen months to build, the first Liturgy being celebrated here on the 1st June 1879. In 1922 the Greek Ecumenical Patriarchate chose St. Sophia to be the Cathedral of the Metropolis of Thyateira and Great Britain, encompassing all Orthodox Christians in the

British Isles and Malta. During World War II the now cathedral became the seat of the Greek government in exile, and therefore also the cathedral of the Greek Nation. The building did not escape bombing but was subsequently repaired. Today there is a small museum in the basement that displays some 19th century treasures and also highlights St. Sophia's links to the local Greek community.

[St. Sophia's Greek Orthodox Cathedral is instantly recognisable on screen by its giant suspended three-dimensional cross]

In *GoldenEye* the Greek Orthodox surroundings of St. Sophia pass very well for the Russian Orthodox surroundings of the church of Our Lady of Smolensk in St. Petersburg, where Natalya meets Boris. The giant overhead iron three-dimensional cross is clearly in shot, the dark and gloomy interior lends a perfect atmosphere to the scene. It should be noted, however, that the exterior shots showing Natalya's arrival were all filmed at Brompton Cemetery Chapel, some three miles away (page 36).

CHARING CROSS* - CHARING CROSS STATION
EMBANKMENT PLACE
MALAYSIA HOUSE
NATIONAL GALLERY
REFORM CLUB

[The Charing Cross Hotel and Eleanor Cross]

The hamlet of Charing, whose name is from the Old English cierran, meaning to turn, was where the road from Bath turned north-west at the

---

* Also served by Embankment Underground station.

point on the riverbank where the river bends. When King Edward I's wife, Eleanor of Castile, died in 1290 at Harby in Nottinghamshire, the funeral cortege rested at twelve places on the journey to Westminster Abbey. The King had crosses erected at each, the Charing Cross being the last. It was made of Caen stone and had Corfe marble statues of Queen Eleanor by Alexander of Abingdon. The cross stood approximately where the current statue of King Charles I stands in Whitehall, but was pulled down in 1647 and some of the stone used to pave Whitehall. Charing Cross is at the heart of London; indeed all mileages to London are measured to here, and it was said that anybody who wanted to know what was going on in London had merely to go to Charing Cross. Doctor Johnson commented that, 'I think the full tide of human existence is at Charing Cross'. The current Eleanor Cross that stands in the forecourt to Charing Cross station is a replica, dating from 1863 and erected at a cost of £1,800 by the South Eastern Railway Company.

The rather cramped station was built on the site of the old Hungerford Market and opened in 1864. It was designed by Sir John Hawkshaw with a single span roof of some one hundred and sixty-four feet spanning six platforms. As the terminus is approached via a bridge over the River Thames, the station is elevated on a brick arched viaduct, varying in height from thirteen feet at the Trafalgar Square end to twenty-seven feet at the bridge end. A year after the station opening the Charing Cross Hotel, designed by Edward Barry, was added giving the station an ornate frontage in the French Renaissance style.

Rather confusingly the station is served by two Underground stations situated at each end of the platforms. At the river end is Embankment, originally called Charing Cross, while the present Charing Cross was Trafalgar Square on the Bakerloo line, and Strand on the Northern line. The latter two were combined to become Charing Cross when the new Jubilee line terminus was opened in 1979. The fact that they were originally separate stations accounts for the long walk between the platforms of the Bakerloo and Northern lines to this day. When the Jubilee line was extended in 1999, it was diverted to Westminster, and the platforms at Charing Cross were closed to the public. The original plan was for the Jubilee line extension to continue along the north bank of the river through Aldwych station, which until 1915 also bore the name Strand. (Aldwych, on a now disused spur of the Piccadilly line, was closed in 1994.)

The former Jubilee line platforms are still maintained, as they are used as a sidings to reverse trains at peak periods, and since the tunnels extend beyond the platforms almost as far as Aldwych they are also used to stable trains. The platforms and tunnels provide an ideal location for film units, as can be seen on screen in *The Fourth Protocol* (1987), *Creep* (2004), *The Deaths of Ian Stone* (2007), *28 Weeks Later* (2007), *The Bourne Ultimatum* (2007), *The Escapist* (2008) and most recently in *Skyfall*.

In the film the first Underground railway reference comes as Q tries to decode some of Silva's computer files. A clue is given by the word Granborough, which Bond says is 'an old tube station on the Metropolitan line'. Bond is almost correct. Granborough Road was the third station north of Aylesbury on a section of the Metropolitan Railway between Aylesbury and Verney Junction that closed in 1936, when the company was taken over by London Transport. Metropolitan Line trains ran to Aylesbury until 1961, when the line beyond Amersham was closed. Granborough Road, on the branch line to Winslow and Verney Junction, was never a tube station, of course, but it is classed with the closed London Underground stations. The track bed is now used for transporting electric pylons, and little remains of the station except part of a platform in the middle of a field.

[The stairs where Silva descends and receives a package in *Skyfall*]

After Silva's escape from MI6 Bond finds himself in a tube tunnel with a train approaching, but manages to go through a service door to the District line, which Q says is the closest. In the next shot Silva is seen descending the stairs from street level into Charing Cross Underground station, where he takes a package containing a police uniform from two accomplices also dressed as policemen. He then heads off towards the booking hall.

James Bond in London

[The Jubilee line platform at Charing Cross, which became Temple and Embankment stations in *Skyfall*]

Bond is next seen searching for Silva at what he tells Q is Temple tube station. This time he is wrong on two counts. First Temple is not a tube station, but an Underground station, and second this is clearly the old Jubilee line platform at Charing Cross. Despite the signs all saying Temple there is a clue to the real location: beneath the signs as Bond walks along the platform are the black and white station murals for Charing Cross, each depicting Nelson's Column. Further, the roof cladding is missing, the panels having been removed at this station due to water leakage problems.

[One of the Charing Cross murals]

Q then instructs Bond, a little belatedly, to get on the Wimbledon-bound train leaving the station, having spotted Silva on board, now dressed as a

92

policeman. There then follows a splendid stunt as Bond races along the platform, passing one of the Nelson's Column murals, and jumps after the train just as it enters the tunnel. Bond manages to grab onto the driver's cab rail, prompting one of the astonished passengers, who presumably doesn't want to go to Wimbledon, to say 'he's keen to get home!'.

This is obviously not a Wimbledon bound train (despite the destination board and a sticker attached to the cab proclaiming that this is the District Line) for as Bond enters the carriage via the driver's cab and continues his search, the vehicle numbers 96069, 96469, 96669, 96269, 96424 and 96114 are clearly in shot, and as any train spotter will confirm these all belong to Jubilee line rolling stock.

[The curved end of 'Embankment' station]

The train appears to pull into Embankment station, though in fact it is arriving back at Charing Cross. This cleverly managed effect is made possible by the fact that the Jubilee line platforms each have a curve at one end, so whereas the scenes at 'Temple' showed the straight section, those at 'Embankment' look in the opposite direction, creating the illusion of a different station.

The chase continues, but the stunt that follows defies logic. Both Silva and Bond are seen sliding down an escalator, though if they are heading for the exit the only way they could go would be up.

[The Northern line escalators at Charing Cross down which Silva and Bond slide. Note the signs in place designed to stop such behaviour]

[Setting up for filming at the bottom of the Northern line escalators at Charing Cross]

There are two sets of disused escalators at Charing Cross, serving the connection with Northern and Bakerloo lines respectively. Those to the Bakerloo line comprise two escalators plus a central stairway, while those for the Northern line comprise three escalators. It was the Northern line access that was used in *Skyfall*. The stunt could have been potentially painful, in the same way that sliding down the banister was for Roger Moore in *Octopussy*, as there are 'stand on the right' signs at intervals between the escalators. Bond leaps over one of the signs at the top of the escalator, but this is the only one we see. The production crew addressed this problem by having Silva land awkwardly at the bottom, sliding along the floor with one of the signs (which he has presumably broken off) beside him.

[The corridor where Silva gives Bond the slip in the crowds (left), although he conveniently leaves the door he uses to exit the station ajar in order that Bond can follow (right)]

The next scene, with Bond looking for Silva among the crowd at Embankment, was also shot at Charing Cross, close to the booking hall seen earlier and the Mad World costume hire shop (where Silva may have got his police uniform!). We then see Silva disappearing through a doorway situated close to Davenports Magic. As no advertising (except for product placement) is allowed in James Bond films all the shop fronts in the arcade were boarded across with panels. Each was imprinted with white tiles so that on screen it looks like one long corridor. Also the yellow access doors were not in keeping with the atmosphere of the sequence and consequently these were also subject to having panels added so as to look as if they were constructed of stainless steel. The final stunt in this part of the film when Silva detonates the bomb that derails the tube train, was filmed back at Pinewood Studios (covered in Volume 2).

The real Embankment station was opened in 1870 by the Metropolitan District Railway (now the District line) as the company extended the Inner Circle (now the Circle line) eastwards from Westminster to Blackfriars. The cut-and-cover construction work was done simultaneously with the building of the Victoria Embankment. The first deep level (tube) platforms were opened in 1906, with the arrival of the Baker Street and Waterloo Railway (now the Bakerloo line), and the second set were opened in 1914 for the Charing Cross, Euston and Hampstead Railway (now the Northern line). The sub-surface District line station was called Charing Cross, but confusingly the Bakerloo line used the name Embankment. In 1914 all the deep level platforms were named Charing Cross (Embankment), and in 1915 the whole station was renamed Charing Cross. What is now the Northern line already had a terminus called Charing Cross (renamed Strand in 1915) at the front of the main line station; the purpose of the extension was to create an easier interchange with the Bakerloo line, whose Trafalgar Square station was, as noted in the previous section, completely separate. South of Embankment the extension ran under the Thames and back again in a loop, with a single platform, which today is the northbound platform. The interchange time was reduced from nearly four minutes to less than two. In the 1920s the loop was abandoned and two new tunnels dug, taking the Northern line on to Waterloo. The loop was hit by a bomb during World War II and flooded, but fortunately it had been sealed off years before.

[The refuse exit to No. 1 Whitehall Place from which Silva emerges]

In *Skyfall* there is a shot of Silva leaving Embankment station after detonating the bomb that causes the Underground train to derail (page 95). However, all is not as it seems, for Silva emerges in Victoria Embankment Gardens where there is no such exit. He is actually appearing from the steps to the basement, where the refuse bins are stored, at No. 1 Whitehall Place (home of the National Liberal Club). All that was added to create this shot was an Underground roundel sign attached to the existing ironwork of the gate.

[Embankment Place, where Silva gets into a police vehicle]

As Silva gets into the waiting police vehicle there is a shot of Embankment Place with another apparent entrance to Embankment station in view. Again this is just set dressing, as it is in real life it is an entrance to Charing Cross station, which has had the signage changed. Finally Silva is seen to speed off down Whitehall Place and left into Whitehall Court.

Embankment was well chosen, more by accident than design, since it was here in 1938 that one of the worst Underground railway accidents took place, when, at around 9.55am on the 17th May, an eastbound Circle line train collided with and eastbound District line train just to the east of the station. Six passengers were killed and forty-three injured. The cause of the accident was not a rogue agent but, it transpired, was due to a signal showing green instead of red, a case of a wrong connection having been made the previous evening when maintenance work had been carried out on the signal.

King Edward I was the first monarch to maintain a mews in which the royal hawks were kept, falconers lodged and daily services held in the Chapel of the Muwes. Chaucer was at one time Clerk of the Mews, and by the time of King Henry VIII they were used as stables. During the Civil War the King's Mews became barracks for the Parliamentary army, and also a prison for up to four-and-a-half-thousand Cavaliers following the battle of Naseby. After the Great Fire of London Wren submitted designs for rebuilding them 'to house three hundred and eighty-eight horses and fifty-two coaches', but the ambitious scheme was never carried out. Instead the east and west sides of the mews were let out to individuals, and in time the main building was used as a menagerie, as well as for storage of public records. In 1830 much of the area was demolished in what was called John Nash's Charing Cross Improvement Scheme.

Nash did not live long enough to see the execution of his plan, which was passed over to Charles Barry. Because the land was on a slope, he built a terrace to the north with a broad flight of shallow steps on either side, leading down to a square. At the foot of the north wall, in the middle, were set out in metal the standard linear measures of the inch, foot and yard.

In 1835 the area was renamed Trafalgar Square, in honour of Admiral Nelson's most famous, and last, victory. The Nelson Column that dominates the square was designed by William Railton. It is of Devonshire granite, Corinthian in form, one hundred and sixty-seven feet tall, with the statue of Nelson by E. H. Baily being sixteen feet in height. The column was erected between 1839 and 1842, the statue being installed in 1843, and the four bronze lions by Landseer added in 1867. At the corners of the square are plinths occupied by King Charles I (facing down Whitehall) and King George IV (in the north-east corner) but the north-west corner was left vacant because King William IV, for whom it was intended, did not leave enough money to finance its erection. From 2001 it was decided that the empty plinth should be used to display modern sculptures in rotation, with each work having a duration of around a year. Between the plinths, on the north side are bronze busts of Admirals Cunningham, Beatty and Jellicoe, while on either side of the Nelson Column are bronze statues of Generals Napier and Havelock. The two fountains and basins were never part of the plans for the square but were added in 1845, and remodelled in 1939 as memorials to Beatty and Jellicoe, with the mermen, mermaids and dolphins only being added after World War II. In 2003 the square was again redeveloped with the pedestrianisation of the north side and the creation of a grand piazza.

Important buildings around the square include the National Gallery (page 100), the church of St. Martin-in-the-Fields, Herbert Baker's South Africa

House, the Admiralty Arch, the former Union Bank at no. 66, Canada House (originally designed by Sir Robert Smirke for the Union Club and the Royal College of Physicians), and the unique former police box, sometimes called Britain's smallest police station, inside a lamp post in the south-east corner of the square.

[The offices of Universal Exports in *The Living Daylights*]

Just south of the square, on the corner of The Mall, is the five-storey building known as Malaysia House. This is not, as some people assume, the site of the Malaysian High Commission (which is actually at Belgrave Square) but offices for the Malaysia Tourism Promotion Board. In *The Living Daylights*, however, this is just a cover for the London offices of Universal Exports.

[Trafalgar Square looking towards the National Gallery]

Along the length of the north side of Trafalgar Square is the National Gallery, which holds the national collection of old master paintings from the 13th century to the beginning of the 20th century. It was founded in 1824 when, during Lord Liverpool's government, the House of Commons voted £57,000 for the purchase of thirty-eight paintings, which had belonged to Russian-born merchant and banker John Julius Angerstein. The paintings were put on display at Angerstein's private house in Pall Mall. At this time two notable collectors, Sir George Beaumont and the Reverend Holwell Carr, came forward offering their paintings for the nation if a suitable building could be found in which to display them. Other donations followed and the national collection soon had two hundred paintings by the likes of Correggio, Titian, Rubens, Rembrandt, Claude, Poussin, Reynolds, Hogarth and Lawrence.

In 1832 construction began on the present National Gallery, designed by William Wilkins, on the site of the King's Mews at Charing Cross, facing south over the newly created Trafalgar Square. The new building opened in 1838 was to increase gradually over the centuries with the growth of the collections. In 1876 a new wing, by E. M. Barry, was added, which includes the splendid dome room with its four chapels. The main staircase and five rooms beyond were a later addition by Sir John Taylor in 1887. With the opening of the Tate Gallery in 1897 most of the British and modern collections left Trafalgar Square, creating more space. In 1911 five more galleries were opened on the west side (where barracks once stood) to balance the Barry rooms on the east side. A northern extension on Orange Street was added in 1975, while the Sainsbury Wing was completed in 1999 to the west of the main building.

[The entrance to the National Gallery used by Bond in *Skyfall*]

The pedestrianisation of Trafalgar Square resulted in the east wing scheme which allowed another public entrance from the square's north terrace (the entrance used by Bond in *Skyfall*). This had the advantage of providing a more direct route from the gallery's lower floor and more space for improved visitor facilities such as the shop and toilets. In 2005 the gallery had in its possession two thousand, three hundred works of art and a floor area equivalent to six football pitches.

In *Skyfall* Bond meets Q, in the form of Ben Whishaw, at the National Gallery, where he is given his new gun, a 'Walther PPK/S nine-millimetre short' which has 'been coded to your (Bond's) palm print so only you can fire it'. As Q says, it is 'less of a random killing machine, more of a personal statement'. Along with this Bond also receives a 'standard issue radio transmitter'. Bond describes his new equipment sarcastically as 'a gun and a radio ... not exactly Christmas, is it?' Q retorts, 'Were you expecting an exploding pen? ... We don't really go in for that any more.'

This sequence was all filmed out of opening hours in the Sackler Room, just in front of Turner's *The Fighting Temeraire*. The room is named after Mortimer Sackler, who died in 2010, and who, having made his money in the pharmaceutical industry in the 1950s and 1960s, became a philanthropist, donating money to the National Gallery for the restoration of the principal British Gallery (Room 34) which was then named after him.

When Joseph Mallord William Turner died in 1851, after an outstanding artistic career, he bequeathed a large number of his paintings to the nation. In his will he stipulated, with a proper appreciation of his own worth, that two of them, *Dido Building Carthage* and *Sun Rising through Vapour*, should be displayed alongside *Landscape with the Marriage of Isaac and Rebecca* and *Seaport with the Embarkation of the Queen of Sheba* by Claude Lorrain, a profound influence on his own work. The will was contested by some of his cousins, on the grounds that his stated condition that the money should pay for an almshouse for elderly artists was illegal. In the event not all of Turner's wishes were fulfilled, but a much larger artistic bequest to the nation resulted – nearly 300 oil paintings and around 30,000 sketches and watercolours, most of which are now housed in the Clore Gallery at Tate Britain.

Turner's will stipulated that the entire collection should be exhibited in a room at the National Gallery bearing his name, but this has not happened. As required, his two paintings were displayed next to Claude's, but it was not until 1861 that all the other finished paintings were displayed together at the National Gallery. Despite the building of an extension, however, shortage of space was always a problem, and in 1910 the bulk of the Turner collection was moved to the new Tate Gallery (now Tate Britain). Among the works retained at the National Gallery were *Dido Building Carthage* and *Sun Rising through Vapour*, which were, as required, hung alongside Claude's paintings, until at the start of World War II the Gallery's entire holdings were evacuated to Wales. After the war, Turner's paintings and Claude's were separated, as the authorities claimed that 'the moral issue raised by the terms of Turner's will is no longer in question,' as he was now recognised as Claude's equal, so 'it would scarcely be necessary for that reason alone to continue the arrangement.' In 1968, however, the four were reunited, and now hang together in Room 15.

Today only ten of Turner's paintings, chosen to represent the full range of his work, are exhibited at the National Gallery. When Q arrives with his equipment, Bond is staring at *The Fighting Temeraire*, a picture that evidently appeals to Q, who says, 'Always makes me feel a bit melancholy. Grand old warship, being ignominiously hauled away for scrap. The inevitability of time, don't you think?' And he asks Bond, 'What do you see?' The reply is, 'A bloody big ship.' HMS Temeraire, a ninety-eight gun ship of the line, became something of a legend for her rôle in the Battle of Trafalgar. She remained in service until 1838, when she was towed from Sheerness to Rotherhithe to be broken up. Turner may have intended his painting to represent the decline of British naval power, the setting of the sun echoing the passing of the old warship, and the little steam-powered tug that tows her being a sign of the future. (In reality, as the vessels are heading westward, the sun behind them should be rising, not setting.) In this late work the paint is laid on thickly to depict the sun's rays striking the clouds, but by contrast the ship's rigging is delicately rendered.

The National Gallery has free admission and is open daily from 10am to 6pm (9pm on Fridays) with the exception of the 1st January and 24th to 26th December when it is closed. For further details please visit www.nationalgallery.org.uk.

With the passing of the Great Reform Bill in 1832 many reformers felt the need for a place to meet in London to counter the Tory Carlton Club. Accordingly Sir William Molesworth announced in February 1835 that a Liberal club would be formed, 'of which the more liberal Whigs, Radicals, etc., will be members'. Further, it was to be 'like the Athenaeum – a good dining club'. It was hoped to attract 'the Reformers of the country to join it, so that it may be a place of meeting for them when they come to town'. However, at a meeting on the 2nd February 1836 it was decided that the Reform Club, as it was to be known, should take 'the best of the Radicals and no Whigs' although Whigs were later welcome to join. The club opened on the 24th May 1836 at Dysart House, No. 104 Pall Mall, next door to the Carlton Club, with a membership of one thousand, a quarter of whom were Members of Parliament. Over time the club became a meeting place, and headquarters, for the fledgling Liberal Party. Later political divisions opened up in the club, the most bitter being over Irish Home Rule between supporters of Gladstone, who favoured such a bill, and the Unionist camp of Lord Hartington who did not. Such divisions eventually led to the club ceasing to be a political one, and by the 1920s it had evolved into an exclusively social one. In 1981 it was one of the first clubs to allow women members. However, it is perhaps best known as where the fictitious Phileas Fogg, the creation of Jules Verne, took on the bet in the club's smoking rooms to go around the world in eighty days.

[Blades where Bond and Graves fence in *Die Another Day*]

The building was designed by Charles Barry and has remained largely unchanged (despite Bond's best attempts in *Die Another Day*!) since it was completed in 1841. It is said to be one of the finest Victorian structures in the country with architecture inspired by the Italian Renaissance. The façade bears a distinct resemblance to the Palazzo Farnese in Rome, which Michelangelo completed in 1589. It is faced with Portland stone comprising nine bays on three floors. Inside there is a vast square atrium which rises the full height of the building, with a glass roof and mosaic floor bearing an Etruscan design. Running along the full length of the rear of the building is the Coffee Room, the traditional name for the restaurant, overlooking the garden. Twenty columns in the Ionic style support the upper gallery from which the Library, Smoking Room and Card Room all lead off. The decoration is described as flamboyant, with large portraits of Whig and Radical leaders in panels, huge mirrors, columns faced with marble and scagliola, richly ornamented and gilded ceilings incorporating elaborate versions of the letter 'R'.

The Reform Club is Blades, where Bond fences with Graves in *Die Another Day*. However, much of what is seen on screen is a studio set, including the exterior, since the garden of the Reform Club is not as large as portrayed in the film and has no fountain. The gallery where Graves damages Gainsborough's famous painting *The Blue Boy* is at the Reform Club, as is the atrium where Bond receives the key to Vauxhall Cross Underground station, and is told by the porter, 'The place needed redecorating anyway'. The club is also seen in *Quantum of Solace* as the building to which M is summoned by the minister to discuss the mysterious Mr. Green. The atrium is again used, this time with the camera angle from above giving an excellent view of the mosaic floor. At the meeting M asks for more time in order to investigate Green, but the minister is of the view that 'if we (the British government) refused to do business with villains we would have no one to trade with'.

The Reform Club may also look familiar from other productions such as *Around the World in Eighty Days* (1956), *O Lucky Man!* (1973), *The Bounty* (1984), *The Avengers* (1998), *The Four Feathers* (2002), *Nicholas Nickleby* (2002), *Scoop* (2006), *Miss Potter* (2006) and *Sherlock Holmes* (2009).

EDGWARE ROAD - THE WATER GARDENS

Edgware Road is a major thoroughfare connecting Marble Arch to, as its name suggests, Edgware in the London Borough of Barnet. Originally it was a Roman road (Watling Street) through the Forest of Middlesex, but today is part of the A5 trunk road. The southern end, noted for its distinct Middle Eastern cuisine and its many late-night bars and shisha cafes, is known variously as Little Cairo, Little Beirut and Little Cyprus.

[The northern tower of The Water Gardens where Mitchell inhabited a flat on the top floor]

Several of the public houses along the road found a new rôle as coaching inns after improvements in 1711 by the Edgware-Kilburn Turnpike Trust, and in the decades that followed Edgware Road became a focus for Huguenot refugees. London's first Indian restaurant was opened there in

1810, and the following year Thomas Telford incorporated the road into the main London-Holyhead route, now the A5. In the late 19th century, thanks to a boom in trade with the Ottoman Empire, there was an influx of Arab migrants, and the trend has continued with Egyptian, Lebanese, Persian and other settlers from the Middle East.

After heavy bombing during World War II the first rebuilding took place at the corner of Edgware Road and Seymour Street, under the auspices of the Victory (ex-services) Club. The Memorial Wing, with shops below, was opened in 1956. However, the most ambitious project for private housing in the area came when the Church Commissioners entered into partnership with Wates, a development company, to restore prestige to the Hyde Park Estate. Under a plan, started in 1957 by Anthony Minoprio, Hyde Park Square was demolished. The new development of 27-acres, on what is now Cambridge Square and Oxford Square, was for nine hundred and thirty flats and sixty-eight houses, with shops and offices to accommodate around four thousand people in all. The corner of the estate between Sussex Gardens and Norfolk Crescent was reserved for total control by the Church Commissioners. They started demolition in 1961 and finished a luxury development called The Water Gardens in 1966. It covers just 3-acres and consists of two hundred and fifty-four flats in three blocks. These new expensive dwellings were quickly occupied. Today this is a private gated community with a manned reception at the entrance to each block.

[Where Bond is seen entering The Water Gardens]

In *Quantum of Solace*, M's bodyguard Craig Mitchell (a double agent) lives in a north-facing flat on the top floor of the northern block.

Bond is driven to The Water Gardens in a black Range Rover, which takes him down the tunnel-like access road to the very end. He joins M in Mitchell's flat, where a fruitless search for clues is under way. Finding an ashtray that she had given Mitchell as a Christmas present, M deliberately smashes it. Bond's comment is, 'I don't think he smoked.'

GREEN PARK* - BUCKINGHAM PALACE SOTHEBY'S

Green Park covers some 47 acres between Piccadilly and Constitution Hill. Unlike London's other Royal Parks, the area is given over almost entirely to grass and trees, without pretty flowerbeds, statuary or other ornamentation. Hence, of course, the name Green Park. Legend has it that the park was once the burial ground for the lepers from the Hospital of St. James, and that this explains the lack of flowers here compared to the adjoining St. James's Park. Green Park was enclosed by King Henry VIII and designated a Royal Park by King Charles II, who had the paths laid out and a snow house built for cooling drinks in the summer. The mound on which the snow house stood can still be seen opposite No. 119 Piccadilly.

During the 18th century the park was a favoured place for duelling, ballooning and firework displays. There was a particularly fine firework display here to celebrate the Peace of Aix-la-Chapelle of 1748, for which Handel composed the incidental music. The largest celebration, though, was in 1814 when a Gothic castle over thirty metres square was erected, with a grand fireworks display from the battlements. When the smoke had dissipated at the end of the fireworks the spectators saw a brightly illuminated Temple of Concord, its walls displaying allegorical pictures, prominent amongst which was *The Triumph of England under the Regency*, standing where the castle had once been. At the same time a balloon rose into the air, piloted by one Windham Sadler, who threw a large number of programmes down into the crowd.

---

* Buckingham Palace is also served by St. James's Park Underground station, and Sotheby's by Bond Street Underground station

Between 1775 and 1856 the Chelsea Waterworks Company had a reservoir in the north-east corner of the park. This is thought to have been where Harriet Westbrook (Shelley's pregnant wife, whom he had deserted) met her mysterious death by drowning in 1816.

The Broad Walk, which cuts across the park from Piccadilly to the eastern end of Constitution Hill, is part of the design for the Queen Victoria Memorial in front of Buckingham Palace.

[Buckingham Palace where Graves is to receive his knighthood]

Buckingham House (as it was originally called) was said to be the most ostentatious private house in London. It was built between 1702 and 1705 for the Duke of Buckingham, whose third wife was an illegitimate daughter of King James II, and who intended it to overshadow King William III's residence, St. James's Palace. This may be why, in 1761, King George III purchased the house from the duke's descendant Sir Charles Sheffield, as a private retreat for Queen Charlotte in place of Somerset House (page 116).

King George IV wanted to demolish Buckingham House and replace it with a palace costing, in 1819, an estimated £500,000, but parliament was only willing to provide £150,000 in funding. The King was stubborn, however, and had John Nash draw up plans, while at the same time he managed to secure a sum that 'might not be less than £200,000' for 'repair and improvement' from parliament. The compromise was that Nash as architect was to retain the outer shell of the earlier house, but even so the costs rose to over £330,000 with the work far from complete. The design was for a three-sided court open at the east, in front of which was to stand the Marble Arch. The two towers at each end were to be square, and there was a central dome in the shape of an inverted egg-cup. In 1828 the Duke of Wellington became Prime Minister. By now Nash wanted to pull down the two wings, which did not meet with the King's approval, but needed more money to continue, which Wellington was not willing to give. However, the work, once begun, could not very well be abandoned, and so yet more funding was forthcoming. The final cost was in the region of £700,000, excluding the cost of the Marble Arch.

The King did not live to see the palace finished. His successor, King William IV, never wanted to live there, and *his* successor, Queen Victoria, was scarcely in residence during the early years of her reign. In fact it was a badly designed building. The drains were faulty; there were no sinks for the chambermaids on the bedroom floors; few of the lavatories were ventilated; the bells would not ring; some of the doors would not close; and many of the thousand windows would not open. Nash was dismissed in 1830 and replaced by Edward Blore, who removed the dome in favour of an attic, and enclosed the courtyard by adding the east front (what most people regard as the main entrance, where the Queen makes public appearances from the balcony). The Marble Arch was also removed from the site where the Queen Victoria Memorial currently stands.

Buckingham Palace comprises some six hundred rooms, only around a dozen being the private domain of the Royal Family. The State Rooms, which include the Throne Room, Ballroom, Dining Room, Music Room, Drawing Rooms and connecting galleries, are open to the public during the summer months. The garden of some 45-acres was landscaped by W. T. Aiton and contains expansive lawns, a lake and a wide variety of trees and flowers (including a mulberry tree originally planted by King James I).

[The Broad Walk gate where Graves gives a press interview]

In *Die Another Day* this is where Graves, who is to receive a knighthood from Her Majesty, lands by parachute in front of Buckingham Palace. He then walks through the ornamental iron gates (a present from the Dominions) at the southern end of the Broad Walk in Green Park as he gives his press conference, before climbing into a black Range Rover and being driven off. It is to be feared that he will be disappointed, since the flag flying over Buckingham Palace is not the Royal Standard meaning that the Queen is not in residence.

James Bond has also visited the Palace for a very special mission, when he was sent to escort the Queen from her residence in order to open the 2012 London Olympic Games, with Her Majesty seemingly parachuting into the stadium from a helicopter, followed by Bond.

The title of chapter six in *On Her Majesty's Secret Service* alludes to the fact that James Bond might well be related to Sir Thomas Bond of Peckham, after whom Bond Street is named. However, this idea is quickly dispelled when Bond confirms that his antecedents were Scottish and Swiss, rather than from South London.

Bond Street was built in two phases, Old Bond Street at the southern end, between Piccadilly and Burlington Gardens, being the work of Thomas Bond in 1684, and the rest of the street (New Bond Street) extending northward to Oxford Street being the responsibility of the Corporation of London in the 1720s. The street was always pretty nondescript and as early as 1736 it was said that 'there is nothing in the whole prodigious length of the two Bond Streets ... that has anything worth our attention'.

It made its name, though, as a luxury shopping street, and in Georgian times it became a fashionable promenade for the *beau monde*, with shopkeepers renting part of their upper floors as lodgings. Among the residents of note were James Thomson (author of the words of *Rule Britannia*), Dean Swift, George Selwyn, Edward Gibbon, William Pitt the Elder, James Boswell and Admiral Nelson. Today the street is still fashionable and a centre for luxury goods such as jewellery, clothes, shoes and luggage. Companies to be found here include Asprey, Cartier Ltd., the Fine Art Society and, at Nos. 34-35 New Bond Street, Sotheby's.

The fine art auctioneers and valuers was established in 1744 by Samuel Baker, a bookseller, who on the 11th March sold 'several hundred scarce and valuable books' from the library of Sir John Stanley for several hundred pounds. From this small beginning he initiated an annual sale until 1754, when he opened a saleroom in Covent Garden where more frequent sales of general objects were held. In 1767 Baker went into partnership with George Leigh, and in 1776 Baker's nephew, John Sotheby, joined the company. On Baker's death in 1778 his estate was divided between Leigh and Sotheby. The Sotheby connection remained for three generations until the passing of Samuel Leigh Sotheby in 1861. It was only in 1917 that the company relocated to New Bond Street and became a serious rival to Christie's as art auctioneers, under the chairmanship of Montague Barlow.

[The main entrance to Sotheby's in Bond Street]

Today the company, which became a public one in 1977, has ninety offices in forty countries, and ten auction rooms with annual sales in the order of £3.6 billion. One of the most dramatic auctions ever held was the sale of the jewels of the Duchess of Windsor in 1987. Held in Switzerland, the sale raised over £30 million. Another dramatic sale was that seen in *Octopussy* when Bond bids for the 'Property of a Lady' in the form of a Fabergé egg. Although unsuccessful in his bid Bond does rather cleverly exchange the genuine article for a fake one which is eventually sold for £500,000 to the villainous Kamal Khan.

[The Fabergé showroom in Grafton Street, just around the corner from Sotheby's, where Kamal Khan might have been able to purchase a replacement Fabergé egg and saved himself a lot of trouble!]

Interestingly Fabergé have a London showroom at No. 14A Grafton Street, at the intersection of Old Bond Street and New Bond Street, just a hundred metres or so from Sotheby's.

OXFORD CIRCUS - THE LANGHAM HOTEL

Oxford Circus, originally called Regent Circus, at the intersection of Oxford Street and Regent Street, is given its circular shape by the quadrants at the four corners, designed with identical facades by Sir Henry Tanner and built between 1913 and 1928. Oxford Street has been a main route to the west since Roman times, though it owes its name to the fact that in 1713 land on the north side was purchased by the Earl of Oxford. It was not then a fashionable area, being described as 'a deep hollow road and full of sloughs; with here and there a ragged house, the lurking place for cut-throats'. Only in the 19th century did the street begin to change, developing into a shopping centre, home to department stores such as John Lewis and Selfridge's, both of which originated here. Oxford Street is full of middle-of-the-market chain stores and cheap market-style complexes. In 1932, Virginia Woolf characterised it as 'too many bargains, too many sales, too many goods marked down ... too blatant and raucous'. Little has changed in that respect.

Regent Street, on the other hand, was part of John Nash's grand plan to connect Regent's Park to Carlton House in Pall Mall. As was pointed out by John Fordyce, the Surveyor-General to the Department of Woods and Forests, the lease on the 500-acre Regent's Park was to revert to the Crown in 1811 at which time the Crown could make profitable developments with the land, but only if there was a road to reduce the travelling time to London. After Fordyce died in 1810 Nash put forward the layout of his street, which was to be a boundary with narrow streets and meaner houses to one side, and squares that the nobility would inhabit to the other. His scheme also included a sweeping curve, the Quadrant, at the Piccadilly end, so as to avoid penetrating the already fashionable St. James's Square. It was to be called New Street, a development by the Crown but dependent upon private capital.

However, such a large project also needed influential patronage which came from the Prince Regent, who was no doubt flattered when it was suggested that the name of the road be changed to reflect his involvement. The original scheme became much altered, but even so by 1819 the Crown started to receive regular rents. By the turn of the 20th century Regent Street had enjoyed eighty years as the centre of fashion in London, and as time went on it was not just where the nobility shopped but where those from the suburbs and country came to shop too. They were a valuable class of customer, although, as one shopkeeper put it, 'one has to do at least five times the volume of business to get the same returns, and even then the net profits are less'. Today the street is still a major shopping centre, and is considered more up-market than Oxford Street thanks to stores such as

Hamley's and Liberty's. At the northern end Regent Street becomes Langham Place, and then Portland Place, before it reaches Regent's Park. Langam Place takes its name from Sir James Langham whose house here was demolished in 1814 to make way for Regent Street. Today three important buildings stand at this curve in the road; Broadcasting House, All Souls' Church and the Langham Hotel.

[The main entrance to The Langham Hotel]

The Langham Hotel was built between 1864 and 1865 to the designs of Giles and Murray. It was the forerunner of London's grand hotels, costing some £300,000, and constructed in the style of a Florentine palace. It had seven floors, six hundred rooms, fourteen thousand metres of carpet, plaster relief ceilings and mosaic floors. It was the hotel where exiled royalty, statesmen, artists, musicians and writers stayed, some of the most notable being Toscanini, Mark Twain, Arnold Bennett, Dvořák, Emperor Napoleon III, Haile Selassie and H. M.Stanley. It was the essence of Victorian pride and respectability. Prior to the Langham being built the land was occupied by a mansion, built in 1767, belonging to Lord Foley. Foley had secured a guarantee from the Duke of Portland, who owned lands to the north, that no building would be erected in front of his mansion so as to obscure his view north to Hampstead. The Duke kept his word, and that is why Portland Place is thirty-eight metres wide, the exact width of the old Foley House, and is one of the most handsome streets in London.

As other luxury hotels opened, mainly to the west, so the Langham declined in popularity. Disaster struck in 1940 when a German land mine hit Portland Place. The hotel was not that badly damaged externally, but its giant water tank was hit, causing major flooding. Between 1965 and 1986 the hotel was owned by the B.B.C. and used as offices, studios and as the home of the B.B.C. Club. The ballroom became the B.B.C. record library, and programmes such as *The Goon Show* were recorded here. After five years redevelopment at a cost of £89 million the Langham re-opened as a hotel in 1991. Since then it has been further redeveloped and extended so that it currently has three hundred and eighty luxury bedrooms, a Grand Ballroom, fourteen other function rooms and a restored Palm Court.

In *GoldenEye* the Langham doubles externally for the Grand Hotel Europe in St. Petersburg, where Bond is staying. The interior scenes were all shot at the studio.

Temple - Somerset House

The area known as Temple lies at the heart of London's legal district. It takes its name from the Inner Temple and Middle Temple, two of the four Inns of Court, which occupy land in the City of London once owned by the Knights Templar. On the other side of the road, in the City of Westminster, are the Royal Courts of Justice. From Temple Underground station, which Bond claims to have passed through in *Skyfall* (though he actually goes no further than Charing Cross – page 89), it is a short walk up Surrey Street to Aldwych.

The old Aldwych Underground station (formerly named Strand) at the top of Surrey Street will be familiar to many film enthusiasts, since it is one of the few stations available for filming throughout the year. Before it was closed in 1994 it was the terminus of a little-used branch of the Piccadilly line from Holborn. Its appearances include *The Battle of Britain* (1969), *Death Line* (1972), *Superman IV: The Quest for Peace* (1986), *The Krays* (1990), *Patriot Games* (1992), *The Good Shepherd* (2006), *An American Werewolf in London* (1981), *Sliding Doors* (1998), *The Black Windmill* (1974) and *Atonement* (2007). Although it looks very much like Vauxhall Cross, where Q has his workshop in *Die Another Day*, all filming in that production was studio based.

In the 7th century there was a Saxon village and trading centre here, called Lundenwic, meaning London market, about a mile upstream from Lundenburh – the London Fort. Lundenwic probably grew up around the mouth of the River Fleet, which served as an anchorage for trading ships and fishing boats. Archaeologists have uncovered evidence of an extensive Anglo-Saxon community stretching along the Strand from Aldwych to the site of Trafalgar Square. It is supposed that when the focus of trade moved to Lundenburh, protected by the Roman walls, the older settlement came to be known as Ealdwic, meaning old market. The name, recorded in 1211 as Aldewich, is now Aldwych.

Aldwych is also the name of the crescent, built at the beginning of the 20th century, connected at both ends to the Strand and to Kingsway at its apex. Its wealth of important buildings include, along the outer edge, the Novello Theatre, the Waldorf Hotel, the Aldwych Theatre, and premises of the London School of Economics. In the centre are India House (the Indian High Commission in London), Bush House (former headquarters of the B.B.C. World Service), and Australia House (the High Commission of Australia). To the south, the church of St. Mary le Strand occupies an island site in the Strand, on the opposite side of which are King's College London and Somerset House.

The original Somerset House was a Renaissance palace built between 1547 and 1550 for Lord Somerset. The entrance gate was carved by Nicholas Cave, King Henry VIII's master mason at Nonsuch. In 1552 Somerset was executed and the property given to Princess Elizabeth, but when she became queen in 1558 part of the house was passed to Edward Seymour, while the rest became a meeting place for the Council, grace and favour residences, and apartments for foreign ambassadors.

In 1603 it was handed to Anne of Denmark, who held many masques here, organised by Ben Jonson and Inigo Jones (who was a resident). After the passing of Anne the house became the property of Prince Charles, although he preferred St. James's Palace. As Charles was to marry a Catholic, a Catholic chapel was added in 1623. Two years later the house was given to Henrietta Maria, and, to compensate her for sending her French attendants home, Charles built her a large new chapel, designed by Inigo Jones. In 1645 she left for the Netherlands and the house was occupied by Members of Parliament and the army. Inigo Jones died here in 1652, and Oliver Cromwell lay in state here in 1658. Soon afterwards parliament decided to sell the house in order to pay the army, but there were no bidders. At the Restoration the house was put in order again and the gallery along the waterfront added. Somerset House was the first English building to have parquet flooring.

[The courtyard close to where Bond helps Wade fix his Trabant]

In 1775 the building was demolished and the site allocated for government offices. What resulted was the imposing building seen today, designed around a large courtyard with a freestanding north wing. As this was before the building of the Thames Embankment, the river used to lap against the south terrace. In 1788 the statue of King George III was erected in the middle of the courtyard, and in 1835 the east and west wings were added. Among the occupants have been The Royal Academy, The Royal Society, The Royal Navy, the Stamp Office, the Inland Revenue and the General Register of Births, Deaths and Marriages.

In 1990, after a comprehensive restoration programme, the Courtauld Institute of Art moved into the north wing, followed in 1998 by the Courtauld Gallery in the Fine Rooms (once the home of the Royal Academy). The Somerset House Trust now oversees the site and with financial aid from the Heritage Lottery Funds has completed the restoration of the south wing and great courtyard (now Fountain Court, since the completion of serried ranks of illuminated water jets which play on the newly laid cobbles). In 2000 both the Gilbert Collection of Decorative Art and the Hermitage Rooms were opened here, though the former has since moved to the Victoria & Albert Museum, and the latter, which staged exhibitions of items loaned from the Hermitage Museum in St. Petersburg, closed in 2007. The Russian connection lives on, however, in *GoldenEye*, where the great courtyard represented St. Petersburg.

In the scene Jack Wade's Trabant has broken down, and he and Bond are seen fixing the car while discussing Janus. The statue of King George III can be seen in the background.

The Bond production team returned here for the next film, *Tomorrow Never Dies*, in which Somerset House doubles for MI6 offices. Bond is seen driving in his Aston Martin DB5 along Strand, turning left through the main gates and entering the great courtyard, having been summoned from Oxford to meet M.

[The Strand entrance to MI6?]

119

Somerset House has also appeared in, among other productions *The Private Life of Sherlock Holmes* (1970), *The Day of the Jackal* (1973), *King Ralph* (1991), *Sense and Sensibility* (1995), *Wilde* (1997) and *The Duchess* (2008).

WESTMINSTER - PALACE OF WESTMINSTER
PARLIAMENT SQUARE
MILLBANK*
WESTMINSTER STATION
WHITEHALL

[The Palace of Westminster]

Westminster itself comprises the area around Westminster Abbey and the Palace of Westminster, the name being self explanatory as the site of the

---

* Also served by Pimlico Underground Station

monastery church to the west of St. Paul's Cathedral. The importance of the area is due to Edward the Confessor, who decided to move his main royal residence from the City of London to a riverside location close to Westminster Abbey, thus separating the commercial centre of London from the seat of royal power and justice. Nothing remains from Edward's time. The oldest surviving part of the Palace is Westminster Hall, built by William the Conqueror's son, King William II. Within the precincts of Westminster Abbey there were many shops, one of which was occupied by William Caxton from 1476 until the printer's death in 1491.

However, the area also attracted less savoury types and was known for its thieves and pickpockets, who would prey on those attending the Royal Court and Parliament, and on pilgrims making their way to Westminster Abbey. It did not help that the Abbey offered sanctuary to fugitives from the law, as streets called Broad Sanctuary and Little Sanctuary remind us even today (just as Thieving Lane indicates the type of person who operated here at this time). By the mid-1800s many of the narrow streets had been demolished and Parliament Square laid out. This encouraged a far better class of citizen, though some would say this did not affect those who actually inhabit the Palace of Westminster on a daily basis!

Until the time of King Henry VIII Westminster Palace was the main residence of the Kings of England, and it remains the administrative centre of the kingdom. The Palace was subject to a fire in 1834, with the only parts to survive to the present being Westminster Hall, the Cloisters (which exhibit some fine fan vaulting and carved bosses) and the Jewel Tower (which was used as a royal treasure house until 1621, when it became a storage place for the House of Lords records). The fire was caused by an act of striking incompetence, when old tally sticks were ordered to be 'privately and confidentially burned'. This they were in the big furnace beneath the Lords' Chamber, and by morning most of the Palace lay in smoking ruins.

The opportunity was taken to rebuild the Palace of Westminster specifically as Houses of Parliament, one condition being that plans should be in the Gothic or Elizabethan style. The winner, out of nearly a hundred designs submitted, was that of Charles Barry and Augustus Pugin, the former providing the practical and commanding plans and the latter the decoration and ornamentation. Construction began in 1837, and the House of Lords was completed in 1847, followed by the House of Commons in 1851 and the Clock Tower in 1858. The finished building was described by James Pope-Hennessy as 'this great and beautiful monument to Victorian artifice', and today it is instantly recognisable the world over as a symbol of London – even of the United Kingdom.

During World War II it was a natural target for bombings and was damaged in eleven separate attacks. Between 1945 and 1950 Sir Giles Gilbert Scott was responsible for having the bomb damage repaired, and also simplifying Pugin's extreme Gothic decoration.

Although there are implied meetings with ministers and the like in several Bond films, no filming has ever taken place inside the building. However, there are establishing shots of the Palace in *Dr. No*, *Goldfinger*, *Die Another Day*, *Casino Royale* and *Skyfall*, while in *For Your Eyes Only* Bond flies past the building in a helicopter during the pre-title sequence, and again goes past in the Q Boat during the chase sequence of *The World Is Not Enough* (pages 137-147).

[Another location for Universal Exports is in Great George Street]

The construction of Parliament Square, designed by Sir Charles Barry in 1868 as a suitable approach to his Houses of Parliament, resulted in the clearance of many slum properties. It was reconstructed in the 1940s by G. S. Wornum but is now little more than a roundabout, although the statues of Lord Derby, Lord Palmerston, Canning, Peel, Disraeli, Field Marshall

Smuts, Abraham Lincoln, Nelson Mandela and Winston Churchill are worthy of note. In *On Her Majesty's Secret Service*, it would appear that this is now the location of Universal Exports since the reflection in the company's brass sign is of Parliament Square. The only building it could possibly be is the side entrance to the old H. M. Treasury Building (now simply known as the Government Offices Great George Street, and housing not just the Treasury, but Revenue and Customs and parts of the Cabinet Office) which extends along Whitehall, Parliament Square, Great George Street, Horse Guards Road (where the current main entrance is located) and King Charles Street. It also extends underground, as this is also the location of the Cabinet War Rooms (which are open to the public), and when the SIS Building is attacked in *Skyfall* (page 49) forcing a move to underground offices it is implied that this is the location. In the film Bond is in conversation with Tanner as they drive over Waterloo Bridge and then enter Smithfield car park (page 74) on their way to the new headquarters, the latter commenting that 'this was part of Churchill's bunker' and that the place is 'quite fascinating if it wasn't for the rats'.

Parliament Square can also be seen briefly in *Skyfall* as M in her black Jaguar is driven around the Square past St. Margaret's Church, on the way to the her meeting with Mallory (page 83).

[Millbank with a distinct lack of traffic of any kind]

Millbank takes its name from the Westminster Abbey mill which once stood at the end of what is now Great College Street. In the 18th century this was a lonely riverside road leading to Chelsea over marshy ground. In 1809 the site, since 1736 occupied by a large house, was demolished to make way for the Millbank Penitentiary, and a decade later houses began to appear along this stretch of road for the first time. Charles Dickens noted that the area was 'a melancholy waste'. By the early 20th century the road was lined with solid Edwardian office blocks with a variety of occupants, such as the Church Commissioners for England, the headquarters for I.C.I. and not least of interest Thames House (the headquarters of MI5). Perhaps the finest building here, though, is the Tate Gallery, built on the site of the former prison, opened in 1897 and named after Sir Henry Tate, the sugar refiner, who not only paid for the building but also provided his own collection of sixty-five paintings to fill it.

On M's return journey from the meeting with Mallory in *Skyfall*, at which she has just been told of her impending retirement, her day gets even worse, as while being driven along Millbank she receives the message on her laptop, 'Think on your sins', just prior to her office being blown up by Silva. For filming, the whole of Millbank between Lambeth Bridge and Vauxhall Bridge was closed off to traffic.

Westminster Underground station is situated underneath Portcullis House, adjacent to Westminster Bridge and opposite the Palace of Westminster and Big Ben (officially named the Elizabeth Tower, to mark the Diamond Jubilee of Queen Elizabeth II in 2012). The station was originally opened as Westminster Bridge in 1868, as part of the Metropolitan District Railway to South Kensington, and remained the terminus for trains until the extension to Blackfriars was opened in 1870. By February 1872 further extensions had been made to the railway system, so that Westminster Bridge was now part of what became known as the Outer Circle line to Broad Street, and later that year, it also became part of the Middle Circle line via Addison Road (now Kensington Olympia). In 1907 the station was renamed Westminster, so as not to be confused with the new Westminster Bridge Road station on the Bakerloo line. A year later the Outer Circle service was withdrawn, but it was not until 1949 that Westminster officially became a station on the Circle line, also served by the District line trains.

In 1999 Westminster also became a station on the Jubilee line. The extension of the Jubilee line necessitated a complete reconstruction, to the designs of Michael Hopkins & Partners. A vast thirty-nine metre shaft was excavated underneath the old station to house the escalators, lifts and stairs to the deep-level Jubilee line platforms. This was in fact the deepest ever excavation in central London, one of the most difficult problems faced by the engineers being the construction of the new station around the existing tracks, without disruption to those services. The tracks had to be lowered by three hundred millimetres, an operation achieved a few millimetres at a time during the several hours that the system was closed each night. The station required by far the most complex engineering of any on the Jubilee line.

[The Parliament Street entrance to Westminster Underground station with Parliament Square in the background. It is from here that Bond emerges and runs up towards Whitehall to save M in *Skyfall*]

The station has a private passageway allowing Members of Parliament and civil servants to access Portcullis House, avoiding public contact. This is one location where an enquiry, such as that in *Skyfall*, may be held. However, in the film Bond is seen exiting the station via the Whitehall exit (though strictly speaking it is Parliament Street) and then running up Parliament Street, but not as far as Whitehall itself, presumably to one of the government buildings here (see next section).

A route connecting Charing Cross to Westminster was first laid out during medieval times. From the 16th century it was a residential street with the likes of Lord Howard of Effingham, Edmund Spenser and Oliver Cromwell living, and in the case of Cromwell dying, here. Whitehall takes its name from Whitehall Palace, which was the chief London residence of the court. King Henry VIII decreed that any persons living there should be 'loving together, of good unity and accord' and should further avoid 'grudging, rumbling or talking of the King's pastime'. It was in Whitehall outside the Banqueting House (the only part of the palace to survive today) that King Charles I was executed on a specially built scaffold. Whitehall Palace was vast, with around two thousand rooms at the time of the Restoration, and a good job too since King Charles II had two of his mistresses, along with the Queen, all living here at the same time.

In 1698 a fire, apparently started by a careless Dutch laundrywoman, destroyed much of the northern end of the road, including most of the palace. By the 18th century there was a move to clear and broaden the street. Whitehall today is dominated by Government offices, including Dover House (Scotland Office), Gwydyr House (Wales Office), the main Ministry of Defence Building, the Department of Energy and Climate Change (at No. 55 Whitehall), the Admiralty Building (now the domain of the Foreign and Commonwealth Office), the Paymaster General's Office, Richmond House (Department of Health), H. M. Treasury Building (including the Old Treasury and Dorset House, Revenue and Customs and parts of the Cabinet Office) and the Old War Office. The Cenotaph, designed by Lutyens and erected between 1919 and 1920, is the United Kingdom's primary war memorial. It is situated in the middle of Whitehall and is the site of the annual ceremony of Remembrance. There are other monuments and statues along the street, mainly with a military theme. Although the whole street is commonly referred to as Whitehall, however, the southern stretch, from the Cenotaph to Parliament Square, is Parliament Street, so not every Whitehall office is actually in Whitehall.

[The Old War Office provides yet another possible location for MI6]

The Old War Office was built between 1899 and 1906 to the designs of William Young. It is in a Victorian baroque style, having four circular towers at the corners to disguise the fact that the plot has no right angles. Inside there are around one thousand rooms and two and a half miles of corridor. In *Octopussy*, *A View to a Kill* and *Licence to Kill* there are establishing shots of this building to imply that it is the location of M's office.

[**The Ministry of Defence building as seen in *For Your Eyes Only***]

Just south of the Old War Office, on the other side of Horseguards Avenue, is the main Ministry of Defence building, as seen in an establishing shot in *For Your Eyes Only*. This huge block was designed in 1913 by Vincent Harris for the Board of Trade, though construction did not start until after World War I and was interrupted by World War II. The building, which can accommodate up to four thousand employees, was finally completed in 1959, at a cost of £5 million. Inside, unexpectedly, are five complete 18th century rooms from houses that previously occupied the site, as well as King Henry VIII's brick-vaulted wine cellar. The main entrance in Horseguards Avenue (and this is what we see in *For Your Eyes Only*) is flanked by Sir Charles Wheeler's thirty-tonne nude sculptures representing *Earth* and *Water*. In 1964 the building was taken over by the newly created Ministry of Defence, merging the previously separate Admiralty (Royal Navy), Way Office (Army) and Air Ministry (Royal Air Force).

[It is on the roof of No. 55 Whitehall that Bond stands admiring the view at the end of *Skyfall*]

Meanwhile, the rather non-descript building immediately to the north of the Old War Office, at No. 55 Whitehall, is presently home to the Department of Energy and Climate Change. Formerly it was the home of the Office of Woods and Forests, and more recently the Department for Environment,

Food and Rural Affairs. It is another building in the Edwardian classical style, designed by J. W. Murray and constructed between 1906 and 1909. Between 1829 and 1890 this was the site of the original Scotland Yard, the first headquarters of the Metropolitan Police.

The roof of the building makes for a memorable scene, as Bond stands alone and isolated, staring over the neighbouring rooftops and fluttering flags of the Old War Office and the Ministry of Defence, in the closing moments of *Skyfall*. It is here that Moneypenny finds Bond and gives him the Churchill pottery dog left to him in M's will, as an indication that he should remain in field work, rather than take a desk job as Moneypenny has done. Immediately following this scene Bond goes to see Mallory, who is now the new M. Presumably, with Silva out of the way MI6 has now come above ground again and relocated to No. 55 Whitehall, while repairs are undertaken at Vauxhall Cross.

Miscellaneous Locations

Hyde Park Corner - Les Ambassadeurs Club

['I admire your courage, Miss …' were the first words said by Sean Connery in *Dr. No* at Le Cercle Les Ambassadeurs, and also where he later says the immortal line, 'Bond, James Bond,' for the first time.]

When Kensington and Knightsbridge were separate from London there was a toll gate at what is now Hyde Park Corner. In the 18th century several schemes were put forward to improve the area. In 1778 Robert Adam proposed a triumphal arch with screens as gateways to the Royal Parks, and in 1796 John Soane envisaged a new palace in the north-east corner of Green Park. With the building of Buckingham Palace in the 1820s it was the triumphal arch that won the day, Decimus Burton designing the Constitution Arch seen here today It was also known as the Wellington Arch as it originally had a somewhat oversized equestrian statue of Wellington on top, which was later removed to Aldershot. The Hyde Park Screen, with carvings by John Herring the Younger, to the north was meant to be an imposing feature of the drive from Buckingham Palace to the park. Today the area is a large roundabout with an underpass connecting Knightsbridge to Piccadilly, as well as a maze of pedestrian subways constructed in the 1960s.

Just behind Park Lane at Hyde Park Corner is Hamilton Place, where at No. 5 is to be found one of the most exclusive gaming clubs in London, Les Ambassadeurs. It has been welcoming society's finest since the early 19th century, and has an unrivalled reputation, as befits a building that has entertained kings and millionaires, politicians and playboys since its earliest days. The current building, dating from 1810, stands on the site of one of King Henry VIII's hunting lodges. The 4th Earl of Buckinghamshire, politician Robert Hobart, was the first inhabitant from 1812 to 1816, followed by an even grander, and more colourful, aristocratic family, the Marquess Conyngham.

The property remained in the family until 1878, when the 3rd Marquess Conyngham sold the house and the family dropped out of the public eye. The following year Leopold de Rothschild bought the house to use as his London residence. He drastically remodelled the mansion to suit his extravagant tastes. The overall style was heavily influenced by *fin de siecle* Louis XV with Renaissance flourishes. The world famous Florentine master wood carver Chevalier Rinaldo Barbetti created the magnificent library and staircase. Equally impressive is the ceiling in the Marble Room depicting *The Four Seasons* by Edmund Parris.

After Rothschild came Captain Leonard Plugge and his wife Anne Muckleston, who lived here until 1950, when they sold the house to John Mills (not the actor). In 1941 Mills had opened the first Les Ambassadeurs Club in Hanover Square. It soon gained a reputation as one of London's most exclusive and distinguished dining clubs, with a membership drawn from aristocracy, diplomats, heads of state, chiefs of commerce and celebrities from the world of entertainment. When Mills moved into

Hamilton Place in 1950 the Club moved with him. Over the coming years Les Ambassadeurs was home to various ventures, including The Milroy Nightclub, The Garrison Club and Le Cercle, one of London's first gaming clubs. When Le Cercle opened in May 1961, exclusively to Les Ambassadeurs' members, it attracted the attention of *The Times*, impressed by the high standard of sophistication and professionalism. Mills ran Les Ambassadeurs until 1981 when it was purchased by casino group London Clubs International, and in turn by the Sampoerna Family in 2006, marking the newest phase in the Club's history.

In *Dr. No* the public are first introduced to James Bond (and Sylvia Trench) as he plays baccarat at 'Le Cercle Les Ambassadeurs London', as the plaque on the wall proclaims. All the interior shots were a film set, but at the time of filming this would have been the newest and most exclusive club in London. Today the annual membership fee is £25,000, so it has to be asked how Bond, on a civil servant's pay, could afford to be a member.

Finally it is worthy of note that John Mills led a fascinating life and may have been a real life James Bond. He was an international businessman, of Polish origin, and was always rumoured to be a government intelligence agent. It is even speculated that Les Ambassadeurs was a front, set up as a testing ground to 'see who could hold their liquor and who spoke freely'.

LEICESTER SQUARE - ODEON LEICESTER SQUARE

The square is named after Robert Sidney, 2nd Earl of Leicester, who purchased four acres of land in St. Martin's Field in 1630. Within five years he had built Leicester House at the northern end and had enclosed the area in front of his large house, thus depriving the inhabitants of St. Martin's Parish of their right to use the previously common land for drying of clothes and the grazing of cattle. An appeal to King Charles I was made, with the consequence that Lord Leicester was ordered to keep part of his land open for the parishioners. This was thereafter known as Leicester Field and later as Leicester Square. In turn Leicester House was to become home to a museum of natural curiosities called the Holophusikon, but it was not a success, and the house was demolished in the 1790s. In 1808 what is now the garden was bought by the Tulk family, who let the area deteriorate to such an extent that by the mid-1850s it was described as 'very ruinous and dilapidated'.

[The Odeon, still the largest single screen cinema in the country]

At the same time there was a protracted legal wrangling as to whether buildings could be constructed in the gardens. This only ended in 1874 when Albert Grant purchased all the outstanding freeholds for £11,060 and promptly donated them to the Metropolitan Board of Works. He also paid for the laying out of the gardens, including the statue of William

Shakespeare at the centre and the busts of Sir Isaac Newton, Joshua Reynolds, John Hunter and William Hogarth (the latter three all having been residents of the square). Today these four figures are situated at the four corner gates. A more recent addition from 1981 is the bronze statue of Charlie Chaplin, in recognition of the square's role as the centre of London's cinema land.

[The Odeon Leicester Square rolls out the red carpet in preparation for yet another film premiere]

It was in the 19th century that Leicester Square first became known as a centre of entertainment, with many amusements peculiar to the era, such as Wyld's Globe, which was built for the great exhibition and housed a giant scale map of the Earth. In 1854 the Alhambra Theatre opened, dominating the east side, and in 1884 the Empire Theatre of Varieties opened to the north. In 1937 a cinema appeared on the former site of the Alhambra Theatre. It consisted of a thirty-seven metre high tower of black polished granite and was built to be the flagship of Oscar Deutsch's Odeon Cinema Circuit.

Indeed, even today it is the largest single screen cinema in the United Kingdom and one of the few with its circle and stalls remaining intact. The cinema is fully equipped to show films in 35mm, 70mm and digital formats on a large screen, as well as having extensive stage facilities for the occasional live show. The cinema still has an operating Compton organ, its console lit from within by coloured lighting, and a safety curtain detailed in 1930s art-deco motifs.

There are one thousand six hundred and eighty-three seats on three levels, along with a circle bar and royal retiring room (which is most necessary, since it is also the location for numerous royal film premieres). In 1967 a refurbishment destroyed many of the art-deco features, though a good number have subsequently been restored, such as the ribbed ceiling and the two bas-relief sculptures of naked nymphs leaping towards the screen from the sidewalls.

No James Bond filming has taken place here, but the Odeon Leicester Square has been the venue for the Bond World Premieres, often attended by royalty, of *From Russia with Love* (10th October 1963), *Goldfinger* (17th September 1964), *You Only Live Twice* (12th June 1967), *On Her Majesty's Secret Service* (18th December 1969), *Live and Let Die* (5th July 1973), *The Man with the Golden Gun* (19th December 1974), *The Spy Who Loved Me* (7th July 1977), *Moonraker* (26th June 1979), *For Your Eyes Only* (4th June 1981), *Octopussy* (6th June 1983), *The Living Daylights* (29th June 1987), *Licence to Kill* (13th June 1989), *Tomorrow Never Dies* (9th December 1997), *Casino Royale* (14th November 2006) and *Quantum of Solace* (29th October 2008).

Dr. No was premiered at the London Pavilion (5th October 1962), *Thunderball* in Tokyo (29th December 1965), *Diamonds Are Forever* in New York (17th December 1971), *Never Say Never Again* in New York (7th October 1983), *A View to a Kill* in San Francisco (22nd May 1985), *GoldenEye* in New York (13th November 1995), *The World Is Not Enough* in New York (19th November 1999), *Die Another Day* at the Royal Albert Hall (18th November 2002) as was *Skyfall* (23rd October 2012).

RIVER THAMES

The origin of the word Thames is obscure, but Julius Caesar refers to the river as the Tamesis, from which the name is derived. Apart from fish for food and water for drinking, a river provides a means of transport and defence. However, a river is also an obstacle that needs to be crossed, either at a ford, or by bridge or tunnel. For the entire tidal stretch of the River Thames there was only one location where both banks had high, dry land of gravel suitable for building a bridge. It was here in Southwark, close to where the current London Bridge stands, that the Roman army built an important crossing, and, naturally enough, over time a settlement grew around the area, which eventually became a port and a crossroads. Here London as a trading city was born, and up to 1750, when Westminster Bridge was built, this was the only crossing of the River Thames in London.

The ownership of the River Thames is an interesting matter, for whereas most rivers in the country are deemed Crown property that right was sold by King Richard I in 1197 for one thousand five hundred marks to a forerunner of the Corporation of London. At that time the sale was only meant to include the fishing and navigation rights, with any revenue going to the Keeper of the Tower of London. The actual area in question stretched from the mouth of the River Medway in the Thames Estuary to Staines near Windsor, and this right was keenly guarded until the mid-1800s. The need for change became apparent in 1836, when a Select Committee reported on the malodorous and general deplorable state of the river. Matters came to a head when the new embankment, which included outfall sewers going directly into the river, was being built some twenty years later. The argument centred on the ownership of the riverbed and the banks upon which the embankment was being built. The dispute went on for seventeen years, with the Crown maintaining that the City of London and the Lord Mayor were only responsible for administering the river. In reply the Corporation of London produced the original documents, which they claimed gave full ownership. Queen Victoria became involved personally in the dispute, and the Crown proceeded by way of Chancery against the Lord Mayor and the Corporation of London. Finally, with the decline in revenue from fishing, because of growing pollution, and navigation, because of the rapid spread of the railways, ownership and management of the River Thames were transferred back to the Crown in 1857.

The river came under the control of the Thames Conservancy Board in 1866, and in 1909 the tidal sections came under the auspices of the Port of London Authority, both of these (along with the Metropolitan Water Board) coming under the single control of the Thames Water Authority in 1974. Certainly since Victorian times the quality of water in the river has improved. For example, the 1980s saw salmon again swimming through central London to their breeding grounds in Molesey, and at the last survey in 2006 there were a reported one hundred and twenty-two species of fish in the river. Much has been done to regenerate the riverside, including the complete redevelopment of Canary Wharf.

The River Thames can of course be seen in many film and television productions, but usually only in the background. Two more recent appearances are in the *Fantastic Four: Rise of the Silver Surfer* (2007) where there is a huge hole in the riverbed beside Westminster Bridge and the London Eye, while the river is also the main backdrop for the marathon in *Run Fat Boy Run* (2007). Finally, a bird's eye view of the river can be seen in the main titles of the long-running B.B.C. television soap opera *EastEnders*.

[One of the Q Boats used in filming *The World Is Not Enough*]

The most dramatic use of the River Thames, though, is in the opening Q Boat chase in *The World Is Not Enough*. In the sequence Bond is seen launching the Q Boat from the SIS Building (page 49) via a torpedo ramp and landing on the river to give chase to Cigar Girl, Renard's accomplice, who is in a sleek Sunseeker Superhawk 34 speedboat. For Bond the production team required a boat that could reach speeds of up to eighty miles per hour and could stay airborne for almost ninety feet. The result was a design by Doug Riddle of Riddle Marine, who constructed a racing machine with a V8 engine. In fact for filming no less than fifteen such Q Boats were built and filmed over a six week period in early 1999.

[The landing stage which Cigar Girl destroys]

Once launched, in fact from the slip way (where the London Duck Tours vehicle is emerging from the water in the picture on page 49) just to the side of the SIS Building, both boats go downriver, with shots of Millbank and the Tate Gallery in the background (page 123). Some nice aerial photography shows them passing the Palace of Westminster (page 120) and under Westminster Bridge (page 54). Cigar Girl now tries to force Bond off the river but ends up crashing into the landing stage by Waterloo Bridge. In fact this was a wholly fake landing stage tethered to the R.N.L.I. Lifeboats station, which can just be seen in shot behind the one destroyed.

So far so good, but the following shots must allow for some artistic licence as the boats are next seen beyond Tower Bridge (which can be seen in the background), St. Katherine Dock and Butlers Wharf, when Cigar Girl evades Bond by turning sharp right (starboard) into St. Saviour's Dock.

[St. Saviour's Dock at low water. Note the depth of the tidemark illustrating that the dock was accessible to large vessels]

This area, Shad Thames, was the largest warehouse complex in London, completed in 1873 to house tea, coffee and spices. The exotic goods are remembered in the names of some of the warehouses (now mostly converted into very expensive apartment blocks): Cayenne Court, Cinnamon Wharf, Cumin Building, Java Wharf, Saffron Building, Saffron Wharf, Tea Trade Wharf, Vanilla & Sesame Court, and the like. Unfortunately St. Saviour's Dock poses a problem for the story. It is a cul-de-sac with a large brick wall at the end, which even the Q Boat could not possibly negotiate.

As if by magic, the next scene shows the two boats emerging from underneath the bridge to the old dry dock at Millwall outer dock on the Isle of Dogs (page 64), opposite Carver's printing works from *Tomorrow Never Dies*, which can be seen in the next shot, as can the Docklands Sailing and Watersports Centre building. This is where the Q Boat comes into its own, as it does a full 360° spin over the now stationary speedboat, destroying the mounted machine gun which Cigar Girl is firing at Bond. This stunt was co-ordinated by Simon Crane.

Cigar Girl turns out to have an even more powerful weapon on board, but though she starts shooting at Bond she only succeeds in blowing up an old

Thames sailing barge. This sequence was filmed some distance away, at the Royal Victoria Dock, easily recognisable by the number of old dockyard cranes in the background. This area has changed rather since filming, not least with the opening of the Emirates Air Line cable car, crossing the river between Emirates Royal Docks and Emirates Greenwich Peninsula.

[The old dry dock at Millwall outer dock from where Bond and Cigar Girl emerge in their boats just prior to the Q Boat's 360° roll (top) and Royal Victoria Dock with ExCel to the left, 'transporter' bridge in the centre and London City Airport in the distance (bottom)]

The Royal Victoria Dock was one of the last to be built, and along with its sister docks (Royal Albert and King George V) make up the largest area of impounded dock water in the world, able to take the largest ocean-going ships of the 20th century. It was constructed by the St. Katherine's Dock Company and opened by Prince Albert in 1855, the spoil not being wasted but taken upriver where it was used to consolidate the marshy land at Battersea Park (to be opened in 1859). The main cargo handled was bulk grain and, later, frozen meat, fruit and vegetables. During World War II it served as a naval and arms base. The Royal Victoria was at the cutting edge of technology for the time, being the first to use the new railways to the full, the first to be designed for steamships, and the first to use hydraulic cranes and lifts for raising ships in a pontoon dock. It closed in 1981 for regeneration over the two decades, in the form of housing, London City Airport (opened in 1987), the award-winning 'transporter' footbridge (1999) and the ExCel Exhibition Centre (2000) on the site of the old Custom House.

[Glengall Bridge close to Crossharbour station under which the Q Boat does a quick dive in *The World Is Not Enough*]

More artistic licence is employed now, as the chase returns to the Millwall outer dock and both boats head north towards the Dutch-style Glengall Bridge in Pepper Street (formerly Glengall Street). Cigar Girl manages to pass through safely before the bridge closes, but Bond is too late, and has to invoke another special feature of the Q Boat. It dives under the surface of the water, while Bond nonchalantly adjusts his tie.

[Two views of Blackwall Basin showing, where the Police launch met its end (top), and the direct route to the O2 under the bridge in the background (bottom)]

In the next scene the geography is roughly accurate. If both boats continue north, passing Canary Wharf on the left, they will find Billingsgate Market, London's wholesale fish market, in front of them at South Dock. From here they can turn right into a canal, passing under Trafalgar Way and into Blackwall Basin, with its residential boats and marina. The basin, whose nearest station is Blackwall, was constructed as one of the entrances to the West India Docks, opened in 1802 as London's first purpose-built commercial docks. Tall ships and steamers passed through here with cargoes of sugar, rum, timber and exotic fruits from the Caribbean. On the south side of the basin is Wood Wharf, which was once lined with timber stores and boatyards. This is where Cigar Girl's boat bisects the police launch that is blocking her way, before continuing in the wrong direction under the Trafalgar Way bridge. Bond soon appears, but as his boat's many remarkable qualities do not include immunity to fire he does not follow Cigar Girl directly. Instead he uses his satellite navigation system to plot a more direct route across the Isle of Dogs peninsula to head her off at the O2. Yet more suspension of disbelief is required here, as the direct route to the O2 is behind him. Blackwall Basin opens into the River Thames immediately opposite the O2, which is clearly visible from it.

[If you park your car illegally on this corner you may get a soaking from a passing Q Boat on its way to Tobacco Dock]

[The 'salmon leaps' that the Q Boat jumps over (top) and Tobacco Dock, taken from where the London Canoe Club building stood before Bond demolished it (bottom)]

The chase takes a momentarily humorous turn now: Bond's boat soaks two traffic wardens clamping a car, as he turns sharply at Asher Way, though this stretch of water is actually some distance upstream, close to St. Katherine's Dock, and moreover is landlocked! The Q Boat then hurdles the 'salmon leaps' ornamental feature along the canal, arriving at Tobacco Dock.

Tobacco Dock was the smallest of the three London Docks, all long since filled in. The name is now applied to the huge warehouse, built in about 1811, that stood beside it. It is a brick building with many vaults and some fine ironwork. At the north entrance is a bronze statue of a boy standing in front of a tiger. This alludes to the wild animal trader Charles Jamrach, who in the late 1800s owned the world's largest exotic pet store close by. One day a Bengal tiger escaped from his shop and picked up a young boy who was trying to stroke the animal. Jamrach chased the tiger and prised open the animal's jaw with his bare hands in order to free the boy, who was unharmed.

The London Docks were closed in 1969, and in 1990 the warehouse was converted into a shopping centre, intended as 'the Covent Garden of the East End'. However, owing to the comparative remoteness of the area, the lack of passing trade and the poor transport links, it lasted only a few years, and use of the building has been sporadic since then. In the summer of 2012 Tobacco Dock housed two and a half thousand soldiers assigned to guard the London Olympic Games, and the building is currently being promoted as London's newest and most flexible conference and exhibition facility. The old ships at Tobacco Dock are clearly in shot as Bond's Q Boat crashes through the London Canoe Club building – but the building is merely set dressing. Neither the club nor the clubhouse actually exists.

We next see the Q Boat crossing Wapping Lane and disappearing down a side-street (actually the entrance, suitably disguised, to the car park of the building opposite). Bond fires the two rear thrusters to continue his journey overland, apparently through Billingsgate Fish Market and into a riverside restaurant, rejoining the River Thames at a spot directly opposite the O2. There would be no point in searching for these locations in London, as the sequence marries scenes shot in the studio and at Chatham (covered in Volume 2). The spot at which the Q Boat leaps into the water is in Jamestown Way, a few yards from Prime Meridian Walk – the brass strip embedded in the pavement to mark the Greenwich Meridian – and as the boat flies through the air, East India Pier is clearly visible behind it. (The nearest station is East India.)

The final stunt, in which the Q Boat soars out of the river to land in a small pond at the O2 (page 24), where numerous display boards advertise the Millennium Experience, was done for real. The pond is still there, in Meridian Gardens, close to the O2 Helipad and North Greenwich Pier.

VICTORIA - EBURY STREET

[Ian Fleming's home at 22b Ebury Street, with an appropriate white Aston Martin parked outside]

The area called Victoria is situated to the east of Belgravia and north of Pimlico. Originally it was part of the Manor of Ebury and recorded in the Domesday Book as belonging to Westminster Abbey. By the 17th century it was part of the Grosvenor Estate and for the next two hundred years was considered nothing more than low-lying unhealthy swampland inhabited by criminals. With the opening of Vauxhall Bridge in 1816, and the Grosvenor Canal in 1825, a series of industrial estates began to appear. In the 1840s and 1850s Thomas Cubitt redeveloped the area. In 1851 Victoria Street cut through the slums, providing fine views of Westminster Abbey and the new Houses of Parliament, and as a consequence many large buildings housing public institutions and shops came into existence. When the canal fell into disrepair, the canal basin became part of the new London, Chatham and Dover Railway, and the terminus, Victoria station, opened in 1862. Today the area is dominated by the railway, Victoria Coach Station, dating from 1932, and Westminster Cathedral (the Metropolitan Church of Roman Catholicism in England).

Ebury Street itself extends from Pimlico Road to Grosvenor Gardens, and was built on land belonging to Ebury Farm in 1820. There have been several famous residents, including Mozart at No. 180, who at the age of eight wrote his first symphony here, George Moore (Irish novelist) at No. 121, Dame Edith Evans (actress) at No. 109, Alfred Tennyson (poet) at No. 42, William Downey (photographer) at No. 57 and No. 61, Vita Sackville-West (author, poet and gardener) and her husband Harold Nicolson (diplomat) at No. 182, and finally Ian Fleming at No. 22b.

The building was constructed in 1830 as a Baptist church, but was later converted into flats. Fleming, who bought his flat from the infamous Oswald Mosley, lived here from 1934 to 1945, and his residence is commemorated by a Blue Plaque. In the novel *Moonraker*, Ebury Street is named as the home of Hugo Drax: 'An hour later passers-by saw a white Mercedes draw up outside a small house at the Buckingham Palace end of Ebury Street.' Later, Bond in his old Bentley pursues Drax, who has Gala Brand hostage in his own car, from Ebury Street towards Dover, but is himself captured by Drax.

JAMES BOND ON LOCATION MAPS

The following maps show the relative positions of the various locations covered in the text. The associated tables give both the type of place, according to the defined symbols below, and the page number in brackets for that location. It is hoped that the maps will help readers in planning their own visits to these places of James Bond interest.

Key to Symbols

🏠	Building (general)	🏛	Building (large/ Important structure)	⛪	Church (religious establishment)
⚜	Military Establishment	🏁	Museum (tourist attraction)	⛰	Natural Feature
🛤	Transport Related				

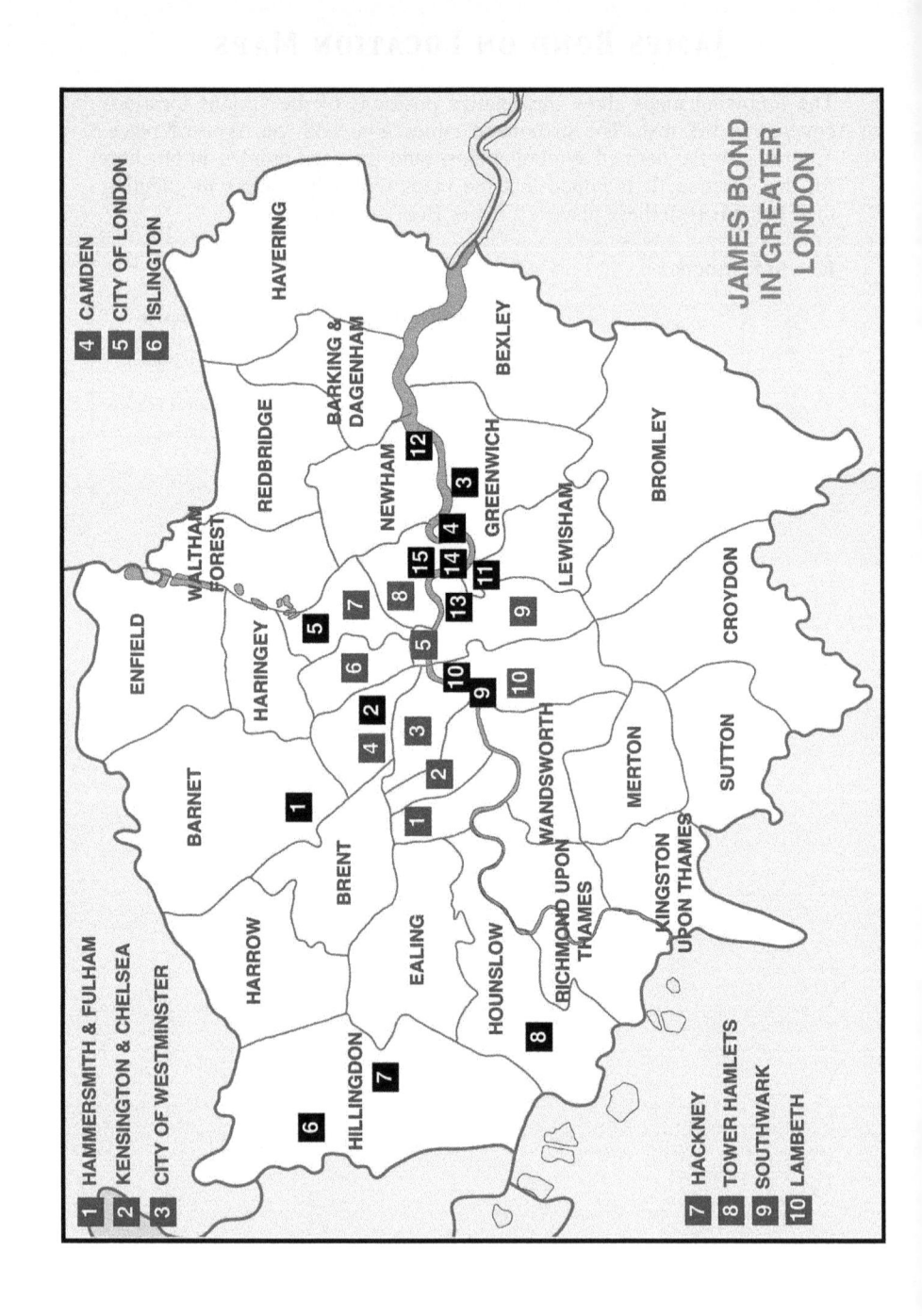

JAMES BOND IN GREATER LONDON

1 HAMMERSMITH & FULHAM
2 KENSINGTON & CHELSEA
3 CITY OF WESTMINSTER
4 CAMDEN
5 CITY OF LONDON
6 ISLINGTON
7 HACKNEY
8 TOWER HAMLETS
9 SOUTHWARK
10 LAMBETH

150

Key to James Bond in Greater London Map

BARNET
| 1 | Brent Cross (13) | |

CAMDEN
| 2 | King's Cross (17) | |

GREENWICH
| 3 | Greenwich (21) | |
| 4 | North Greenwich (24) | |

HACKNEY
| 5 | Stoke Newington (26) | |

HILLINGDON
| 6 | Harefield (28) | |
| 7 | Ruislip Gardens (29) | |

HOUNSLOW
| 8 | Feltham (34) | |

LAMBETH
| 9 | Vauxhall (44) | |
| 10 | Waterloo (51) | |

LEWISHAM
| 11 | New Cross (57) | |

NEWHAM
| 12 | Gallions Reach (58) | |

SOUTHWARK
| 13 | Canada Water (62) | |

TOWER HAMLETS
| 14 | Crossharbour (64) | |
| 15 | Westferry (66) | |

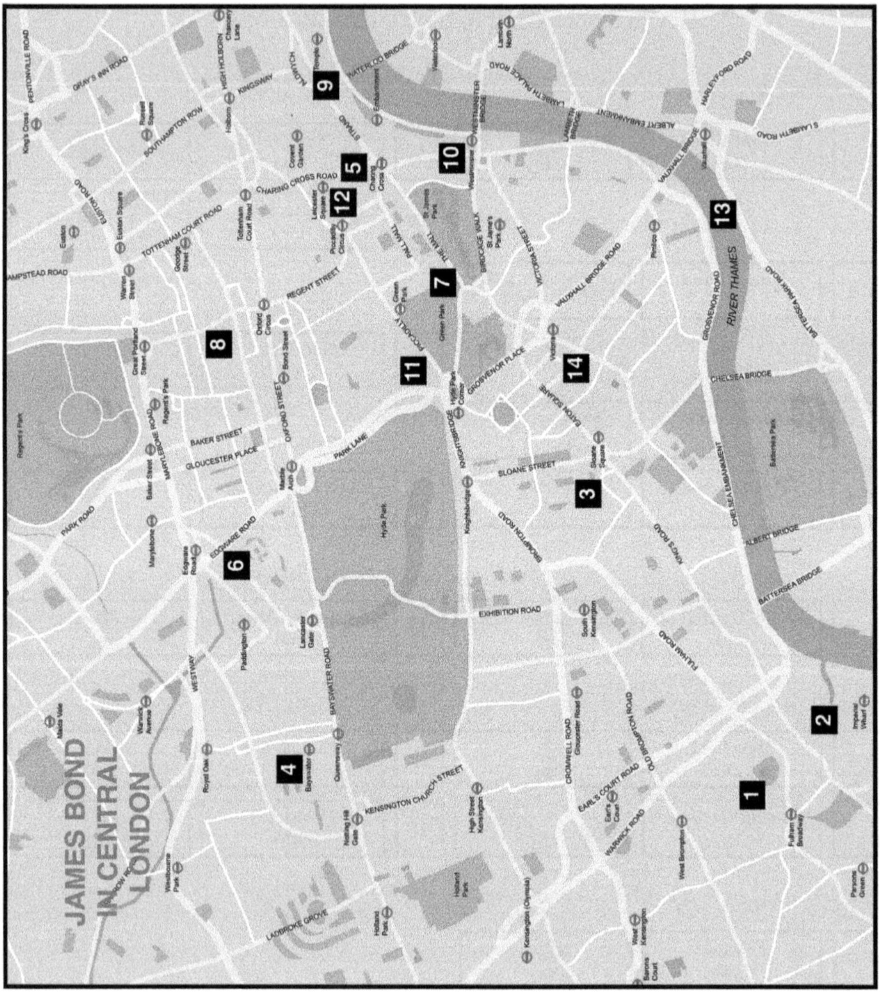
JAMES BOND IN CENTRAL LONDON
RIVER THAMES
HYDE PARK
PARK LANE
OXFORD STREET
REGENT STREET
BAKER STREET
KNIGHTSBRIDGE
SLOANE STREET
KING'S ROAD
CHELSEA BRIDGE
ALBERT BRIDGE
BATTERSEA BRIDGE

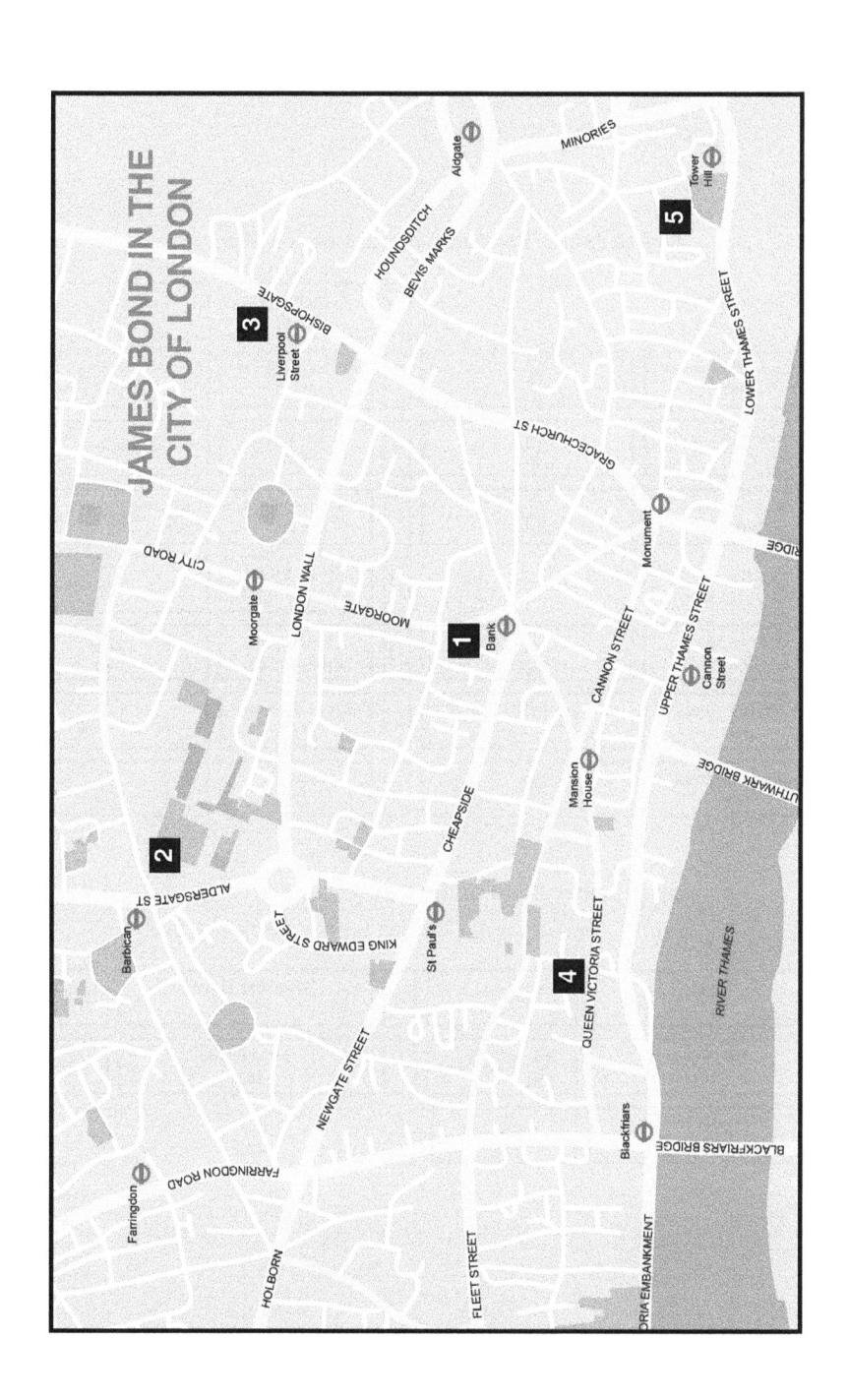

JAMES BOND IN THE CITY OF LONDON

Key to James Bond in Central London Map

	KENSINGTON & CHELSEA				
1	Fulham Broadway (36)		7	Green Park (108)	
2	Imperial Wharf (38)		8	Oxford Circus (114)	
3	Sloane Square (40 & 42)		9	Temple (116)	
	CITY OF WESTMINSTER		10	Westminster (120)	
4	Bayswater (86)		11	Hyde Park Corner (131)	
5	Charing Cross (89)		12	Leicester Square (133)	
6	Edgware Road (105)		13	River Thames (137)	
			14	Victoria (147)	

Key to James Bond in the City of London Map

	CITY OF LONDON				
1	Bank (67)		4	Mansion House (79)	
2	Barbican (70)		5	Tower Hill (83)	
3	Liverpool Street (76)				

Places Index

Buildings or Places in General
Cadogan Square 40
Canary Riverside Health Club 66
Ebury Street 147
Embankment Place 95
Henniker Mews 43
Kingsland House 26
Les Ambassadeurs Club 131
Old Vic Tunnels, The 51
Parkside Business Estate 57
Snake Ranch Studios 38
Water Gardens, The 105
Wellington Square 42

Churches & Other Ecclesiastical Buildings
Brompton Cemetery Chapel 36
St. Sophia's Greek Orthodox Cathedral 86

Large or Important Buildings and Structures
Albert Embankment 44
Beckton Gas Works 58
Bedfont Lakes Office Park 34
Brent Cross Shopping Centre 13
Broadgate Tower 76
Buckingham Palace 108
College of Arms 79
Drapers' Hall 67
Harmsworth Quays Printing Limited 62
Langham Hotel, The 114
Malaysia House 98
National Gallery 100
Odeon Leicester Square 133
Palace of Westminster 120
Port of London Authority Building 83
Reform Club 103
Smithfield Market 74
Somerset House 116
Sotheby's 111
Vauxhall Bridge 47
Vauxhall Cross 49
West Ferry Printers 64
Westminster Bridge 54
Whitehall 126

155

Places Index

Military Related
R.A.F. Northolt 29

Tourist Attractions
College of Arms 79
National Gallery 100
O2, The 24
Old Royal Naval College 21
Palace of Westminster 120
Somerset House 116

Transport Related
Charing Cross Station 89
R.A.F. Northolt 29
St. Pancras Station 17
Westminster Station 124

Miscellaneous
Frobisher Crescent 70
London Wall 72
Millbank 123
Parliament Square 122
River Thames 137
Summerhouse Lane 28

Film Index

Dr. No (1962)
8, 45-47, 122, 131, 133

From Russia With Love (1963)
8, 42, 136

Goldfinger (1964)
7, 8, 17, 29, 31, 122, 136

Thunderball (1965)
7, 31, 136

You Only Live Twice (1967)
8, 136

On Her Majesty's Secret Service (1969)
8, 20, 42, 53-54, 56, 73-74, 82-83, 111, 122-123, 136

Diamonds Are Forever (1971)
8, 136

Live and Let Die (1973)
7, 44, 136

The Man with the Golden Gun (1974)
8, 136

The Spy Who Loved Me (1977)
7, 8, 136

Moonraker (1979)
9, 42, 136, 148

For Your Eyes Only (1981)
7, 59-61, 122, 128-129, 136

Octopussy (1983)
7, 24, 32-34, 113, 127, 136

Never Say Never Again **(1983)**
7, 136

A View to a Kill **(1985)**
8, 127, 136

The Living Daylights **(1987)**
7, 8, 41, 100, 136

Licence to Kill **(1989)**
127, 136

GoldenEye **(1995)**
8, 13, 20, 38, 39, 50, 69, 89, 116, 118-119, 136

Tomorrow Never Dies **(1997)**
13, 15-17, 34, 63, 65, 73, 119, 136, 140

The World Is Not Enough **(1999)**
9, 26, 34-36, 64, 122, 136, 138-147

Die Another Day **(2002)**
8, 13, 27, 48, 50, 54, 56, 104-105, 110-111, 122, 137

Casino Royale **(2006)**
7, 8, 41, 122, 136

Quantum of Solace **(2008)**
70, 72, 105, 107-108, 136

Skyfall **(2012)**
7, 8, 9, 13, 24, 41, 49, 50, 53, 57-58, 66, 74, 75, 79, 84, 86, 91-95, 96, 101-103, 116, 122, 123, 124, 125-126, 129-130, 137

ACKNOWLEDGMENTS

The author and publisher are delighted to be able to thank all those who have supported this publication from its inception.

With the exception of those listed below all photographs in this book were either already in the public domain, or were taken by the author. Our thanks is given to all those who have graciously given permission for their photographs to be used here.

Borough of Newham (page 60), Dr. David Brown (page 49), Can Stock Photo Inc. (gun barrel image), The Drapers' Company (page 69), Foster + Partners (page 47), Koenig & Bauer Group (page 63), London Underground Film Office (pages 91-94), The National Motor Museum at Beaulieu (Bond in Motion exhibition) (pages 33 and 138), The Old Vic Tunnels (page 51) and Photoshot (Daniel Craig image).

Special thanks goes to Stephen Norris who has given his boundless knowledge and advice freely in all aspects of this book, and also to Graham Rye (editor, designer and publisher of 007 Magazine) for his input, along with Roger Johnson for his editing and proof reading skills. In alphabetical order the following are also thanked for their generous time, advice and expertise: Nick Bishop (The Drapers' Company), Dr. David Brown, Tony Burlton (Landmarc Support Services Limited), Dr. Heather Chisholme, Shirley Cody (London Underground Limited), Paul Curtis (tfl), Lucy Faulks (The Old Vic Tunnels), William Hunt (Windsor Herald, College of Arms), James Richards, Squadron Leader Richard Willis (R.A.F. Northolt) and Sarah Wright (Beaulieu Enterprises Limited).

References used in the research of this book (and highly recommended to those who would like to explore the themes of this publication further) include:

Cork, John & Stutz, Collin, *James Bond Encyclopedia*, 336 pages, Dorling Kindersley Limited, (2009), ISBN: 978-1-40534-430-2.

Giblin, Gary, *James Bond's London*, 171 pages, Daleon Enterprises Inc., (2001), ISBN: 978-09713-133

Mulder, Martijn & Kloosterboer, Dirk, *On The Tracks of 007*, 287 pages, DMD Digital, (2008), ISBN: 978-0-97131-330-9.

Acknowledgments

Weinreb, Ben (Editor) & Hibbert, Christopher (Editor), *The London Encyclopaedia*, 1120 pages, MacMillan Reference, (2010), ISBN: 978-1-40504-925-2.

Finally, at a corporate level gratitude goes to EON, Danjaq, United Artists Corporation, Columbia Pictures Industries, Sony, MGM, the Ian Fleming Estate and of course the late Ian Fleming himself for originally creating the character of James Bond without which this publication would not exist.

**THE END OF *JAMES BOND ON LOCATION*
VOLUME 1: LONDON**

**BUT *JAMES BOND ON LOCATION* WILL RETURN
IN VOLUME 2 DEDICATED TO THE
REMAINING UNITED KINGDOM FILMING LOCATIONS**